D1095639

PSYCHOANALYSIS
OBSERVED

Psychoanalysis Observed

GEOFFREY GORER

ANTHONY STORR

JOHN WREN-LEWIS

PETER LOMAS

Edited with an Introduction by
Charles Rycroft

COWARD-McCANN, Inc.
NEW YORK

CONTENTS

Introduction:
Causes and Meaning

CHARLES RYCROFT

WHEN this volume was first suggested its provisional title was *Objections to Psychoanalysis* and it was to have been included in the *Objections* series, in previous volumes of which churchmen, both Anglican and Catholic, and humanists have discussed critically their own beliefs. It soon became apparent, however, that the choice of this title was based on a false analogy, since it assumed that psychoanalysis is a 'belief' in the sense that Christianity and humanism are, and that analysts are the priests and theologians of a new religion—a view to which no analyst could be expected even to appear to subscribe.

The title *Objections to Psychoanalysis* also begged an important question, since one of the unsolved problems about analysis is precisely its logical and metaphysical status; and to have assumed in the title that it is an ideology would have precluded at the outset discussion of what sort of an animal psychoanalysis really is, whether it is a religion, as some of its critics assert, a science, as most of its practitioners claim, or an art, a craft, one of the humanities, a form of semantic theory —or even something *sui generis*, a new phenomenon which eludes classification into any of the traditional categories.

It therefore seemed better to abandon the idea of *Objections to Psychoanalysis* and start afresh by inviting a number of persons who have been in close intellectual and professional contact with psychoanalysis, whether as practitioners themselves, like Dr Lomas, Dr Storr and myself, or as workers in related fields, like Mr Geoffrey Gorer in social anthropology and Mr Wren-Lewis in theology and industrial science, to discuss psychoanalysis in the form in which they have themselves encountered it.

My own contribution should be read as an overture which introduces some but not all of the themes which are developed in the four main essays; that of Cure being elaborated by Dr Storr, that of Cause and Meaning by Dr Lomas in his essay on Freudian and existentialist analysis, that of the analyst as an authority on sex and child-care by Mr Geoffrey Gorer, and that of Psychoanalysis, Science and Religion by Mr Wren-Lewis. All four essays were, however, written independently of my Introduction and of one another and combine to form a conspectus of psychoanalysis today, of its place in the world, and of its prospects and potentialities, which is both more detailed and more panoramic than could have been achieved if it had been observed through a single pair of eyes.

In this context psychoanalysis is to be understood in its wider meaning to include all 'psycho-dynamic' theories and therapies, regardless as to whether they emanate from Freud or Jung or elsewhere. Although the Freudian professional organizations regard the term 'psychoanalysis' as one which refers solely to their own theory and practice, and although the Jungians and Adlerians call themselves analytical and individual psychologists respectively in the hope of differentiating themselves from the Freudians, these distinctions have never caught on even among the well-informed laity, which has always been more impressed by the similarities of the schools than by their differences.

In England, too, the attempt to reserve the term 'psychoanalysis' for Freudian theories has been rendered absurd by two local developments: the emergence of Kleinian analysis which claims to be Freudian and is yet disowned by many Freudians but received sympathetically by many Jungians, and the close personal relations existing between individual Freudians and Jungians which has resulted in a number of Jungian analysts having become analysands of Freudians and vice versa. The picture is further complicated by the existence of the existentialists, who certainly belong to the movement of thought begun by Freud but who reject many of his basic premisses.

Throughout this book, therefore, psychoanalysis, unless specifically qualified, should be taken to refer to all those theories and therapies—whether Freudian, Jungian or existentialist—which assume the existence of unconscious mental processes, which concern themselves with the elucidation of motives and which make use of trans-

ference—and which can be differentiated from the
organic school of psychiatry and from behaviourism
(learning-theory) by the fact that they regard subjective
experience as a central object of study and not as an
awkward contaminant which has to be either ignored or
eliminated.

When I first became an analyst it seemed to me that
the idea of applying the scientific method to psychological phenomena was a perfectly straightforward
matter and that there were no particular difficulties
about regarding unconscious wishes or infantile com-
plexes as causes of which present-day conscious symptoms were the effect, or in assuming that if a patient
became aware of the unconscious and infantile determinants of his symptoms, these would vanish; and,
indeed, even today I frequently have clinical experiences which can readily be understood in this way.

But, and it is a big but, these experiences only occur
with a certain type of patient and under certain conditions. They occur with patients who are basically
healthy and whose personality neither the therapist nor
the patient feels inclined to call into question, and they
occur only if both the patient and his nearest and nomin-
ally dearest wish him to lose his symptoms. In other
words the patient loses his symptoms only if two conditions are fulfilled : firstly, that he understands their
origin, and secondly, that his conscious wish to lose his
symptoms is greater than his wish to retain the *status
quo* in his personal relationships. For instance, if a married man is impotent or sexually perverted, his recovery
depends not only on his understanding of the origin of
his disability but also on whether his wife really and

truly welcomes his recovery, and on whether, if she doesn't, he feels prepared to overcome her reluctance or, if that seems impossible, to make alternative arrangements. Whether he does feel prepared to do either will depend on many more factors than the unconscious determinants of his symptoms: it will be influenced by his conscious values, his religious attitudes, his general feelings towards his wife, his assessment of her mental stability, etc.

I am really making three points here. Firstly, symptoms are not solely an individual matter, they have a social nexus and function and change in one person may be contingent on changes in others. Secondly, in patients other than straightforward psychoneurotics, analysis involves consideration of the whole personality including his conscious values. And thirdly, conscious as well as unconscious motives play a part in the maintenance of neuroses.

The last point raises the question as to whether conscious motives can be regarded as causes. Although there are, it seems to me, no difficulties about regarding unconscious 'wishes', 'motives' and 'causes' as synonymous, particularly when the 'effect' being considered is a symptom which is alien to the patient's personality, it is much more difficult to maintain that they are interchangeable ideas when applied to conscious phenomena. Once any mental process or group of ideas becomes conscious it becomes part of the whole complex of thoughts, feelings, wishes, values and aspirations which constitute the personality, and one of the characteristic functions and activities of the personality is making decisions. Although a neurotic cannot decide to become potent or to lose a fear of crowds, and his symptoms are therefore the effect of forces and ideas of which he knows nothing, the healthy person (and the neurotic in healthy and unaffected parts of his life) spends much of his time deciding whether or not to do things that he wishes to do or feels he ought to, and his decisions are influenced not only by the strength of his own wishes and principles but also by his estimate of the likely effects of his actions on himself later and on those around him. It would seem indeed that one of the functions of consciousness is to enable decisions to be made, and the idea that all conscious decisions are strictly determined by unconscious forces seems to imply that all deciding is an illusion and that consciousness has no function—which is unlikely. A more probable hypothesis is that consciousness transmutes instinctual drives in such a way that the outcome of any act of decision is NOT solely determined by the relative strength of the instinctual forces involved.

Although this latter assumption is one which could be used to retain the notion of unconscious causation in a psychology which took account of conscious motives—and is indeed so used by the American school of psychoanalytical ego-psychology[43] [44]—it is not in fact the assumption which Freud made when he propounded his principle of psychic determinism. Freud's aim was to establish a "scientific psychology" and he hoped to be able to do so by applying to psychology the same principles of causality as were in his time considered valid in physics and chemistry. As a young man his own teachers in physiology had held that it was inadmissible to explain the working of the human body by reference to principles other than those which could be derived from physics and chemistry, and as a result they rejected all vitalist biological theories. Freud's grand design was to adopt the same attitude towards the working of the mind, and he believed that his discovery of unconscious mental forces made his project attainable. If, he argued, all mental activity is the result of unconscious mental forces which are instinctual, biological and physical in origin, then human psychology could be formulated in terms of the interacting of forces which were in principle quantifiable, without recourse to any vital mental integrating agency, and psychology would become a natural science like physics.[50]

However, the principle of psychic determinism remains an assumption, and one which Freud made out of scientific faith rather than on evidence, and I know of no instance in Freud's writing of his claiming to have predicted in advance the outcome of any choice or decision made by a patient. Indeed, when describing the causes of neuroses, he more than once repudiated the idea that it is possible to predict whether a person will develop a neurosis or, if he does, what kind of neurosis it will be. All he claimed was that in retrospect it is possible to assert that such-and-such an event or situation in childhood had been the cause of the neurosis; a procedure which is more reminiscent of a historian than of a scientist.

He did however claim, and successfully claim, to be able to demonstrate that choices made by patients are not arbitrary and that they can be understood as revealing and characteristic manifestations of their personality. For instance, in his *Introductory Lectures*[27] Freud describes how he asked a womanizing male patient to tell him the first female name that came into his head. The man did so, producing a name which was not that of any of the many women he knew, but was very similar to Freud's nickname for him. Now, Freud does not claim to have predicted this name—indeed he describes himself as having been as surprised by it as the patient was—but he saw immediately its similarity to the patient's name, and this did not surprise him, since he had already appreciated that the man was not a great lover of women, but a narcissist.

What Freud did here was not to explain the patient's choice causally but to understand it and give it meaning, and the procedure he engaged in was not the scientific one of elucidating causes but the semantic one of making sense of it. It can indeed be argued that much of Freud's work was really semantic and that he made a revolutionary discovery in semantics, viz. that neurotic symptoms are meaningful disguised communications, but that, owing to his scientific training and allegiance, he formulated his findings in the conceptual framework of the physical sciences. In some aspects of his work Freud saw this himself clearly. His most famous work he entitled *The Interpretation of Dreams*[21] not *The Cause of Dreams* and his chapter on symptoms in his *Introductory Lectures* is called *The Sense of Symptoms*.[28] He was also well aware that many of his ideas had been anticipated by writers and poets rather than by scientists.

The idea that psychoanalysis is not a causal theory but a semantic one is not original. It has been propounded in America by T. Szasz in his *Myth of Mental Illness*,[80] in which he argues that the idea that the neuroses are diseases with causes is a social fiction which is outgrowing its usefulness, and in England by James Home in his paper 'The Concept of Mind'.[45] It is also held in different forms by the existentialists. But it is not orthodoxy, and the majority of Freudian analysts disclaim it entirely. They thereby lay themselves open to attack from critics like Professor Eysenck who see quite clearly that psychoanalysis cannot satisfy the canons of those sciences which are based on the experimental method but who believe that if they can demonstrate its inadequacy as a causal theory, they have proved that it is nonsense.[16] [17] To my mind, one of the merits of the semantic view of analysis is that it completely undercuts the Eysenck–Psychoanalysis controversy by showing that both parties are not only, as Eysenck himself has said, arguing from different premises but from wrong premisses. On their side the analysts are claiming that analysis is what it is not, and, on his, Eysenck is attacking it for failing to be what it has no need to claim to be. And both parties are assuming that it is only the physical sciences which are intellectually respectable. It is perhaps relevant here, that for very different historical reasons, both psychology and medicine are faculties which suffer from an inferiority complex in relation to science.

Recognition of the semantic nature of psychoanalytical theory would also undercut the tendency of analysts to engage in futile controversy as to whether the cause of neurosis is to be found in the first three months or years of life, or whether the fundamental cause of neurosis is constitutional envy of the mother's breast or is to be found in the Oedipal phase of childhood or in the infant's sensitivity to environmental impingements, and enable them to concentrate on improving their techniques for getting into communication with those who have become alienated for whatever reason.

There is, of course, one type of neurosis which undoubtedly does have a cause, and this is the traumatic neurosis which occurs after a totally unexpected shock, but this is precisely the neurosis which does *not* fit into psychoanalytical theory, and one of its symptoms, the traumatic dream in which the shocking experience is relived, provides the one example of a dream which is not amenable to analytical interpretation. Freud evidently regretted this, since in his last book, *An Outline of Psychoanalysis* (1940)[35] he wrote of the traumatic neuroses: "their relations to determinants in childhood have hitherto eluded investigation".

It does, of course, remain possible that all the neuroses might be explained as similar to the traumatic neuroses, in that they could be seen as responses to specific pathological and unsatisfactory childhood experiences, though it is worth noting that Winnicott, the English analyst who has been most persistent in tracing the origin of neuroses to environmental failures in early childhood, has also found it necessary to introduce the distinction between a 'true' and a 'false' self. But 'true' and 'false', like the 'authentic' and 'inauthentic' of the existentialists, are semantic and evaluative concepts, not scientific, causal ones. Perhaps the principle of psychic determinism applies to the 'false self', while the 'true self' has free will.[84]

Preoccupation with the idea of causality has led analysts into the position of giving advice and making recommendations about matters on which, to my mind, they only appear to be experts. If, so the argument runs, neurosis is the result of infantile traumata and deprivation, then it could be prevented by parents caring for their children better, and analysts have therefore come to regard themselves, and to be accepted, as experts on the upbringing of children. Both in this country and more particularly in America, a literature exists which contains advice on such matters as how and when infants should be weaned, how the births of children

should be spaced, when and whether they should be
punished, and even on how parents should love their
children, the authority for such advice apparently
deriving from psychoanalysis. Now although much of
this advice is probably as wise as advice emanating from
other sources, it tends in fact to derive from paediatric
and child-guidance experience, and much of it is open
to objections of three kinds.

Firstly, the idea that children should be treated lov-
ingly and humanely is one that does not require any
scientific, medical or psychological backing and can be
arrived at without reference to psychoanalysis or, indeed,
any other body of knowledge.

Secondly, loving is not an activity which can be
engaged in on advice, since its essence is sincerity and
spontaneity.

And thirdly, much of the trauma and suffering en-
dured by children is unavoidable. It is really no use saying that children should not be separated from their
parents and need their full-time love and attention up
to such-and-such an age, when the facts of human existence are such that no parent can guarantee to remain
alive for the requisite number of years after becoming
one, or even that he or she will go on loving the other
parent for so long. As a result much of this sort of
advice is both sentimental and perfectionist and may
even, on occasion, be harmful, since it may encourage
parents to be insincere out of a sense of guilt or duty. It
may also induce a sense of guilt in parents who, through
no fault of their own, have to bring up children under
difficult and unsatisfactory conditions. Many of our
patients are the offspring of tragedy, not of faulty child-
rearing.

The idea that neurosis is caused by lack of love in

childhood can also lead analysts into priggishness. If neurosis is the result of parental deprivation then perhaps analysis is a form of replacement-therapy and the effective agent in treatment is the analyst's concern, devotion and love. But this view of the matter leaves unexplained why the analyst should consider himself to be the possessor of a store of *agape* or *caritas* so much greater than that of his patients' parents. Analysts who hold that their capacity to help patients derives from their ability to understand them, and that this ability depends on their knowledge of the language of the unconscious, are really being more modest. The claim to possess professional expertise does not contain a concealed claim to moral superiority over the laity.

If psychoanalysis is recognized as a semantic theory not a causal one, its theory can start where its practice does—in the consulting-room, where a patient who is suffering from something in himself which he does not understand confronts an analyst with some knowledge of the unconscious—i.e. who knows something of the way in which repudiated wishes, thoughts, feelings and memories can translate themselves into symptoms, gestures and dreams, and who knows, as it were, the grammar and syntax of such translations and is therefore in a position to interpret them back again into the communal language of consciousness. According to the scientific analyst this can only be done by elucidating and reconstructing the history of the illness and of its infantile origins, but even he agrees that this is useless unless the analyst has made contact (*rapport*) with the patient, and it seems to me that it makes better sense to say that the analyst makes excursions into historical research in order to understand something which is interfering with his present communication with the patient (in the same way as a translator might turn to history to elucidate an obscure text) than to say that he makes contact with the patient in order to gain access to biographical data. In the former he is using the past to understand the present, in the latter he is using his biographical research to legitimize his *rapport* with the patient by formulating it in terms of a theory about the causes of neurosis. Furthermore, as the conditions of analytical work make it inconceivable that any analyst, or even group of like-minded analysts, will ever encounter a representative sample of any particular neurosis and as, indeed, the validity of particular neurotic diagnostic categories is open to doubt, since neuroses are in a sense personal creations, such research is in any case methodologically suspect.

There is, however, a form of research which not only can be done by analysts but is indeed done by all analysts regardless of whether they consider themselves research workers or not. This is research into the private languages of patients and of the ways in which their cryptic and disguised utterances and gestures can be understood and translated back into common and communicable language. This is research in exactly the same sense that linguistic research is. An analyst encountering a new patient is in a position surprisingly similar to that of a linguist who encounters a community which speaks an unfamiliar language. To get his bearings he explores how much language they have in common, listens to him and by locating the contexts in which initially incomprehensible utterances occur and referring back in his own mind to other languages he knows, he gradually learns his patient's language, and makes himself familiar with his imagery and style of thought and feeling.

If he is not theoretically minded he will leave it at that, in the same way as some people who have a gift for languages may learn to speak them without ever acquiring an interest in grammar and linguistic theory. His research will then increase his own insight and clinical competence but will not be communicated to anyone who does not come into direct contact with him as patient, pupil or colleague. The late John Rickman, who would, I suspect, have agreed with much of this essay, often used to remark that much that is valuable in psychoanalysis is handed on not in learned papers but by verbal tradition.

If, on the other hand, he is theoretically minded, he will formulate the language-patterns he has learnt, will relate them to those he has previously encountered or which have already been described in the literature, and will write clinical and theoretical papers. To continue the linguistic analogy, diagnosing a patient as suffering from hysteria or obsessional neurosis is like locating a language as belonging to a particular family, while general analytical theory is analogous to general language theory. The basic principles of the language theory applicable to dreams, verbal imagery and physical gestures have already been formulated by Freud in his *Papers on Metapsychology*[26] where the grammar and syntax of the unconscious is stated in terms of the primary processes (condensation, displacement, etc.) and in the analytical literature on symbolism.

Here again I must disclaim originality. The idea that what Freud described as characteristics of the unconscious or Id is better thought of as the grammar of an unconscious, nonverbal language is to be found in, for instance, Erich Fromm's *The Forgotten Language*[36] and Tauber and Green's *Prelogical Experience*,[81] though neither of these are books which I would endorse in their entirety.

The statement that psychoanalysis is a theory of meaning is incomplete and misleading unless one qualifies it by saying that it is a *biological* theory of meaning. By this I mean that psychoanalysis interprets human behaviour in terms of the self that experiences it and not in terms of entities external to it, such as other-worldly deities or political parties and leaders, and that it regards the self as a psychobiological entity which is always striving for self-realization and self-fulfilment. In other words, it regards mankind as sharing with the animal and plant world the intrinsic drive to create and recreate its own nature. Part of the resistance among analysts to the idea that psychoanalysis may be a semantic theory derives from the fact that the concept of meaning is felt to have both religious and political overtones. Freud himself dismissed the problem of meaning by asserting that anyone who questions the meaning of life is ill. By this he can, I think, only have meant that living itself gives meaning to life and that this is doubted only by those who have become to some measure self-alienated, and who as a result have recourse to religious or ideological theories of meaning as a 'secondary construction', an attempt to restore the lost sense of meaningfulness by deriving it from some source external to the self. This was, I suspect, the real basis of his antagonism to religion. For him, religion was a cosmology, its central notion being a God who was outside the universe and who had created it. As a scientist, he realized that the traditional Judeo-Christian cosmology was no longer tenable, and he therefore interpreted religion as an illusion which those who needed it created for themselves in order to preserve the childhood illusion of being absolutely protected and loved by a father. However, in interpreting religion as a neurosis, as a defence against anxiety and feelings of helplessness, he was himself applying a theory of meaning, since he made sense of it to himself by ascribing to it a function in the lives of those who believe it and one with which he could himself empathize.[32]

Recent developments in theology, however, make it very doubtful whether cosmology can be regarded as the central religious idea or whether belief in a God 'out there' is the essence of the religious attitude. Although we can have no idea of what Freud personally would have made of Bonhoeffer's "religionless Christianity", or of Zen Buddhism, or of statements like Guntrip's[41] "the fundamental therapeutic factor in psychotherapy is more akin to religion than to science, since it is a matter of personal relationship... religion has always stood for the good object relationship", there would seem to be no necessary incompatibility between psycho-analysis and those religious formulations which locate God within the self. One could, indeed, argue that Freud's Id (and even more Groddeck's It),[40] the impersonal force within which is both the core of oneself and yet not oneself, and from which in illness one becomes alienated, is a secular formulation of the insight which makes religious people believe in an immanent God: if this were so, psychoanalysis could be regarded as a semantic bridge between science and biology on the one hand and religion and the humanities on the other. This was what I had in mind at the beginning of this essay when I listed as one possible answer to the problem of psychoanalysis's metaphysical status, the possibility that it might be something *sui generis* which could not be fitted into any of the traditional categories.

Psychoanalysis in the World

GEOFFREY GORER

I

IN the first decade of this century, it is reliably reported, when Sigmund Freud was a little-known neurologist in Vienna, and only the foundations of the theory and practice of psychoanalysis had been laid, colleagues with some personal difficulties in their private lives used to come to Austria-Hungary to ask Freud for assistance with their problems. This assistance was freely given; Freud would take the colleague in distress for a long walk in the Prater. In the course of that walk the colleague would describe his symptoms, his memories of his early childhood and one or two recent dreams. On the basis of this information, Freud would make a diagnosis of the trauma or traumata from which his colleague was suffering and communicate it; at the end of the walk the colleague's psyche would be analysed and the insight he had been given would (it was confidently hoped) prevent the recurrence of the symptoms which had hitherto disturbed him.

Freud himself did not retain a belief in the value and validity of instant diagnosis and insight-giving for very long; by the end of the First World War psychoanalytic treatment had approximated to its present form and duration, and diagnosis without the month-long process of psychoanalysis was considered worthless, indeed almost a betrayal of the principles of psychoanalysis. But for some reason which I am unable to explain, those early walks in the Prater (which were private and only referred to in psychoanalytic gossip) seem to have been very influential in the picture of psychoanalysis as a therapeutic process as portrayed in popular films and novels. In these, typically, two or three dreams are described or depicted, the patient may tell a little of his, or more frequently her, childhood and, aha! the analyst, like a benevolent magician, exorcizes the horrid experience from the past, the memory of something nasty in the woodshed; all difficulties disappear and the road to love and success is smooth and open.

The image of the psychoanalyst as a benevolent exorcist is probably the most widespread favourable view of the therapist; and indeed it has held some attraction for some analysts, including Freud himself who discussed cases of medieval possession,[31] and W. R. D. Fairbairn who consciously used the metaphors of demonology.[18] The most widespread fear of psychoanalysts among the lay public seems to be that of a malevolent magician who will set free the destructive forces of lust and violence previously held in bondage by the 'strength of character' produced by educational training and (often) religious principles. Both images represent the psychoanalyst as a man with uncanny powers.

Most psychoanalysts would argue that the excessive hopes and fears felt by sections of the public concerning the uncanny powers of psychoanalysts were unrealistic projections of their unconscious wishes; and in many individual cases this is most probably true. But psychoanalysts are to a certain extent responsible for this overestimation of the powers of psychoanalysis; quite a few of the books by psychoanalysts intended for a lay public imply that psychoanalytic theory gives them an insight into matters of general concern of a depth and quality which are simply not available to the uninitiated, to people without their qualifications.

At first these implicit claims to possess the key to the scriptures, the hidden wisdom, were advanced in quite modest little essays about works of art and literature whose 'true' meaning, ignored by critics over the centuries, could be made clear by the application of psychoanalytic insight. What was odd about these essays by Freud,[25] Ernest Jones[49] and many others of the original group of psychoanalysts is that they treated poets' or artists' creations *as if* they were real people. They discussed Hamlet as if he were a patient, not a character in a play; Moses' thoughts—not Michelangelo's—were evoked as an explanation of the contradictions in the statue's pose. Implicitly, writers and artists were treated as though they were entranced mediums issuing communications from the 'beyond' or manifesting a secondary personality. These communications had been admired by the critics and amateurs of art and literature for the wrong reasons from the moment they became available until the psychoanalyst turned his attention to them; his uncanny insight disclosed what people had really been admiring, which was very different to what they had thought.

It was a small step from works of literature to mythology, especially as Freud had used the myth of Oedipus as a metaphor for his fundamental discovery of the ontogenetic phases of development in European male children.* With a little more justification than in the case of works of art, mythology was treated as if it existed in its own right; after all, almost by definition myths have no authors. While they are treated as valid they are recounted or represented in certain settings before an audience; but this setting and the audience were not considered by the psychoanalysts. Their insight could show what was the 'real' meaning of the myths, again very different from what the carriers of the myths had supposed.

It would not be too much of an exaggeration to say that the quarrel, and eventual schism, between Freud and Jung and their followers developed from the alternative techniques of explaining the 'real' meaning of myths. For Freud and the Freudians they are in the final reduction metaphors of unconscious wishes and fears, to be explained in the same fashion as the manifest content of dreams (but with no reference to a dreamer); they all refer to the human body and its functions or to the small nuclear family. For Jung and the Jungians myths are veiled statements of transcendental truths about the nature of the universe; the same transcendental truths can be elicited from individual dreams; but

---

* In *Totem and Taboo*[24] Freud applied this metaphor to the phylogenic development of mankind. The data he used have never been acceptable to professional anthropologists.

for them it is the myth which validates the interpretation of the dream, not (as with the Freudians) the interpretation of dreams which reduces the myth to human comprehensibility.

Myths are, or were, the religious beliefs and stories of people distant in space or time, of pagans and primitives; but if other peoples' beliefs and legends can be interpreted by the application of psychoanalytic insight, why should our own be immune? They were not for long; further essays were written to show that Christianity, Judaism and monotheism were illusions, projective systems to be understood and explained away like all other myths; or, by the Jungians, to be understood as distorted versions of the Universal Truths inherent in all religions.

There is little evidence to suggest that these psychoanalytic essays on religion have had any considerable impact on the climate of opinion in Europe or the U.S.A. The agnosticism (or atheism) of Freud himself and of the majority of Freudians differed only in degree from that current in the intellectual circles likely to read the essays. The mysticism of Jung and his followers may have persuaded some people (including, oddly enough, some Protestant clergy) that there was a 'scientific' foundation for their amorphous and heterodox religious yearnings; but it seems improbable that the writings of psychoanalysts on religion have been even marginally effective in influencing either the 'decline' of religious belief or the increase in religiosity in any country. What is noteworthy is that some of the specialists in a system of therapy have shown no hesitation in making pronouncements on a subject about which they (with few exceptions) have neither specialized knowledge nor experience. If the lay public tend to credit psychoanalysts with uncanny powers, the claims of some psychoanalysts to have the final answers to problems which have exercised Western man over recent millennia must be held in part responsible for this overestimation.

Fewer psychoanalysts have made pronouncements on politics; but those who have written on political subjects have written with the same assurance of having access to wisdom denied to ordinary mortals as have the writers on religion. The grossly psychopathic character of most of the leading Nazis and of their ideology rendered them suitable subjects for psycho-diagnosis at a distance; but writers as dissimilar as Erich Fromm[37] and Roger Money-Kyrle[69] have appeared to claim that psychoanalytic training and practice are adequate equipment for prescribing the political conduct of nations. The two writers quoted are in agreement that political life would be improved if people were more rational and less under the sway of unconscious forces, and that psychoanalysts are uniquely qualified to prescribe what is rational; but their prescriptions agree in very few particulars. Unless one grants their basic assumption that the practice of psychoanalysis automatically bestows wisdom and knowledge inaccessible to the profane, their political analysis and preferences do not appear to have more logic and cogency than those of many other political pamphleteers with a different training.

Psychoanalysts, by reason of their training and study, are uniquely qualified to understand, analyse, and assist the patient on the couch; but as soon as they move away from this personal confrontation (or the modification of a small group) to comment on matters outside their training and experience, the value of their comments would appear to depend on their knowledge and wisdom, not on their qualifications.* Freud was a wise man and his views were hardly ever without interest, even when he was building constructs on very slender or unsatisfactory data; and the same has been true of a few of his followers; but too many have rashly followed his example in extrapolating their psychoanalytic concepts on to subjects for which they have no special qualifications. Although these reflections spiced with a psychoanalytic vocabulary have rarely had any wide circulation, their existence may have added to the hopes or fears of uncanny knowledge which, I have suggested, many of the lay public feel.

II

An important component in many schools of magic or esoteric knowledge is the employment of Words of Power; these Words gives the user control over occult forces. For many people—perhaps more in the United States than in Britain—some of the vocabulary of psychoanalysis and of general psychiatry (to the extent that the two vocabularies do not overlap) has acquired some of the characteristics of Words of Power. Many people appear to feel that when they have applied a psychoanalytic or quasi-psychoanalytic term to a person or situation they have somehow gained control of the person or situation, rendered it or him understandable, safe, innocuous. Among these Words of Power in cur-

* A partial exception should be made for those psychoanalysts who have studied dead people as if they were patients, using all the available documentation. Ella Sharpe on Shakespeare,[77] Marie Bonaparte on Edgar Allan Poe[5] or Erik Erikson on Luther[13] have, I would consider, added to our knowledge of these people in a way which they could not have achieved without their psychoanalytic qualifications.

rent use 'inferiority complex', 'paranoid', 'infantile', 'narcissistic', 'sadistic' and 'masochistic' seem to be the most comforting.

A potentially dangerous use of these Words of Power is the communication of a psychoanalytic diagnosis to a disturbed person. The best-documented example of this misuse of psychoanalytic diagnoses known to me is Dr William Sheldon's *Varieties of Delinquent Youth*;[78] a surprising number of his 200 young criminals from Boston could give a correct (or at least plausible) psychoanalytic diagnosis of their own character and problems, diagnoses which had been communicated to them by the social workers assigned to them by the courts after their earlier brushes with the law. That this communication of diagnosis without treatment is not confined to the social workers of Boston is suggested by the song 'Gee, Officer Krupke' from the musical, *West Side Story*.

I think most practising psychiatrists (not only psychoanalysts) would agree that the communication of a diagnosis without therapy is unhelpful in itself and runs the risk of making any therapeutic treatment which is subsequently undertaken more difficult and prolonged (by providing the patient with further 'defences'). One can only suppose that the social workers were engaged in a magical act when they uttered these Words of Power and communicated them to the young criminals. If these criminals had been possessed by devils such exorcisms might have been effective.

One of the areas in which the diffusion of psychoanalytic concepts has been most influential in much of Britain and the United States is in the increasingly widespread beliefs that delinquents are 'sick' or 'maladjusted' (two more Words of Power) rather than criminal, and that therapy is more appropriate than punishment. Since these beliefs are probably conducive to compassion and gentleness on the part of the authorities directly dealing with criminals, their diffusion on the balance is to be welcomed; but they are founded on relatively little cogent evidence and the system of values from which they derive has been relatively little scrutinized.

Freudian psychoanalytic theory is basically historical, accounting for the development of any adult character by the vicissitudes which that person has experienced since birth; it treats learning as cumulative, so that early experiences influence later experiences. Together with Freud's other discoveries concerning the development of infancy and early childhood, this makes the experiences of the first six years of life extremely influential in the development of later character; anybody's current behaviour can be, at least in part, explained by these early experiences.

Theoretically, everybody's character, however admirable or deplorable, is accountable to the same extent from the vicissitudes of infancy and early childhood;* but in the context of delinquency or anti-social behaviour it is only the inadequate whose misconduct is explained, and explained away, by reference to earlier mishandlings or misfortunes. Thus, to take a very generally accepted situation, whenever the family backgrounds of a group of delinquents or other social misfits are investigated, it is found that a large number come from

* My colleagues and I have made considerable use of this theoretical construct in our studies of 'national character' or 'personality-in-culture', by attempting to isolate the varying treatments of infancy and early childhood which are normative in different societies.

'broken homes'; and it is often argued that 'broken homes' are the 'cause' of delinquency. But when a population is sampled on some other statistical basis and their family backgrounds are also studied, it is found that 'broken homes' occur in the background of the best adjusted in the same proportion as they do in the maladjusted.* I do not know of any sampling which has been able to tabulate the occurrence and influence of the other demons of psychiatric penology, the over-possessive mother and the rejecting mother, for these qualities are far harder to determine satisfactorily from a short interview or questionnaire; but if such a study could be made, I should be surprised if the results were not analogous to those for 'broken homes'.

The application of concepts more or less directly derived from psychoanalysis are above all exculpatory: 'It's not my fault I'm a bad boy; it's the way my Mum treated me.' But, logically, if it's not my fault I'm a bad boy, it's not my virtue if I'm a good one; but I know of no studies to show people are not *really* responsible for their heroism or piety, their diligence or their integrity. Psychoanalytically tinged explanations are invoked for the failures, not for the successes.

Although this position is logically untenable, it may have some social advantages in the justification of compassion which outweigh its disadvantages of sloppy thinking and the rejection of responsibility for their own actions by those delinquents and other maladjusted people who have learned how to use the Words of Power deriving from psychoanalysis.

---

* The most impressive documentation of this fact occurs in the late Dr S. Stouffer's massive study of *The American Soldier*;[79] but the same result has been replicated for smaller samples in several British and American studies.

III

As Freud implied in his essay *The Antithetical Meaning of Primal Words* (1910),[23] Words of Power can be used to bless as well as to curse, to invoke as well as to exorcise. The psychoanalytically-tinged words which seem to carry the greatest positive aura today are 'adjustment' and 'maturity'. 'Adjustment' seems a relatively simple concept: working effectively and not being consciously unhappy in whatever situation the individual finds himself. In the words of the hymn, 'He made them high and lowly, and ordered their estate'; and the 'well-adjusted' man or woman is contented in the estate ordered for him or her. But 'maturity', when the word is divorced from a chronological and developmental frame of reference, is to me a very puzzling concept. It is used, with undertones of approval, in a wide variety of contexts; but it is difficult to find any common connotations in the uses of this word except that it is a mark of approval for the present or the past and an aspiration for the future. As such, it seems to have much the same function in psychological or psychoanalytic discourse as 'double-plus' had in the Newspeak invented by George Orwell for *1984*.[71]

Very frequently the term carries hidden self-commendation; those who praise or advocate 'maturity' always seem to consider that they themselves possess or exemplify this quality; in many cases it could be paraphrased as 'those who think, or feel, or act in this situation in the same way that I do'. Although this paraphrase would be easier to understand, it would not carry the same aura of a 'scientific' standard of values.

In a specifically sexual context 'maturity' would seem to mean staying married and enjoying marital intercourse. In this sense it would appear to be a less disturbing synonym for the older psychoanalytic ideal, the 'genital character'. As far as I can understand the concept, the 'genital character' was not necessarily married but was heterosexual, had frequent intercourse and did not change partners often; but 'maturity', at any rate after the end of physiological adolescence, does seem to imply a legally sanctioned marriage. Of course, if one's spouse is 'immature' it may be necessary to get a divorce before pairing up with a 'mature' partner. The 'genital character' perhaps reflected the middle- and upper-class sexual mores of Central Europe before 1914; the 'mature personality' would then reflect the sexual mores of contemporary middle-class Britain and the United States.

I think there can be little doubt that the current consensus that frequent, satisfactory, heterosexual intercourse is desirable in itself and an essential component of adult human happiness derives from and is supported by the diffusion of ideas and values closely linked with Freudian psychoanalysis. Although the common disparagement of (Freudian) psychoanalysis that it is 'obsessed by sex' or 'traces everything to sex' can easily be demonstrated to be partial and inaccurate, Freud and his followers did create a climate of opinion and a vocabulary in which sexuality could be discussed without embarrassment or furtive excitement and which made the pleasure which most human beings feel in this activity a good which could be publicly acknowledged.

But this change in the climate of opinion has taken place in the English-speaking countries in societies where the puritan ethic is still a major component in the superegos or consciences of the majority of their members. The Pursuit of Happiness was very easily changed

34

from a right to a categorical imperative; the guilt which, the evidence suggests, was formerly felt for too great an indulgence in the carnal lusts of the flesh has now been transferred to under-indulgence. A person who does not achieve, or—worse still—does not get pleasure in an adequate frequency of intercourse is likely today to suffer from all the feelings of inadequacy, of un- worthiness, of shame that his or her ancestors might have felt for their excessive fleshliness even sixty years ago.

Sixty years ago Lord Curzon could state without sur- prising his audience or the people who repeated his aphorism : 'Ladies don't move'; and in most middle- class circles in Britain and the United States a respect- able woman who enjoyed intercourse would have kept this a close marital secret. In many circles bachelors and spinsters were admired for their 'strength of character'; and men or women who were found to be conducting extra-marital liaisons were shunned and whispered about.

Today the situation is almost completely reversed in the parallel social circles. Those with a conspicuously successful sex life are admired and envied; the celibate are likely to be shunned and whispered about. Then the libertines were looked down on for their 'weakness of character' and possibly contaminating effect; today the celibates are looked down on, suspected of perversion or treated as 'maladjusted' and 'immature'. This change of attitude is surely related to the diffusion of ideas of mental health deriving from various dilutions of psychoanalysis.

It is plausible—though statistically impossible to prove —that this change of values has resulted in some in- crease of individual happiness and charity, on the assumption that in the English-speaking populations a higher proportion of the population are temperamentally licentious than are temperamentally celibate; in such a case fewer people are having to counter their temperamental inclinations or suffer from feelings of guilt and unworthiness today than they did two generations ago. Since very little is known about the distribution of temperaments within any society, this assumption can only be a guess; in the contemporary climate of opinion the suggestion that there exist temperamental celibates would be rejected without examination.

The argument for assuming that such temperaments do occur derives from historical and anthropological evidence. Whenever societies have developed institutions for the celibate—predominantly those societies where unreformed Christianity or unreformed Buddhism were or are dominant religions—these institutions do not appear to have had difficulty in recruiting voluntary celibates to maintain their numbers. Quite probably, some young people were forced against their inclinations into the monasteries, nunneries and their equivalents; but observation in contemporary Buddhist societies suggests that this is not a major source of recruitment.*

The temperamental celibates (if such exist) are probably made unnecessarily unhappy by the transforming of the Pursuit of Happiness into an ethical imperative, with sexual implications. Another group of people also rendered unnecessarily unhappy and insecure by this system of values are those women who cannot achieve a sexual orgasm. The evidence strongly suggests that the capacity to achieve sexual orgasm is closely related to female genital anatomy. Within a heterogenous population some women have the conformation which makes

* Celibacy, whether religious or secular, is uncommon in societies which have not achieved a relatively advanced technology. The lack of surplus produce and a sanctioned division of labour based on sex can probably account for this.

orgasm spontaneous, some have the physical capacity to acquire it as a learned pattern, whereas for some it will be permanently physically impossible. It is this last segment of the female population who now risk being made to feel unhappy, unworthy and inadequate; if their husbands or lovers are conscientious, they will feel unworthy and inadequate too. The current cultural imperative demands that every woman should have an orgasm at every act of intercourse; if she fails, she is frigid (today probably the most damaging adjective), perverse or 'immature'.

Anthropological evidence suggests that the female orgasm is a cultural option. I am employing the phrase 'cultural option' to indicate that societies vary in the use they make and the value they accord to various physiologically based capacities which seem to occur sporadically in most or all moderately large populations, but whose evolutionary significance is obscure. Other examples, besides female orgasm, are perfect pitch and trance. In societies without formalized music or singing, perfect pitch would presumably be unrecognized either by the possessor or the rest of the population. In societies with formalized music, perfect pitch may be considered an idiosyncratic gift which may be admired in all or only in people of one sex or age; or it may be little valued. There are societies, however, which demand that everybody should be able to sing in tune, such as Bohemia in the eighteenth century or traditional Wales in more recent years; in such societies the tone-deaf presumably suffer from feelings of worthlessness and inadequacy. The capacity to go easily into trance may be valued in one or both sexes as a sign of supernatural grace and an ability to get in touch with the gods or to prophesy; it may be despised (as in our own society) as a sign of mental instability and 'immaturity' or feared as possession by an evil spirit. In societies where the capacity to go into trance is valued, the number of those with spontaneous capacity may be considered insufficient and techniques will be developed to teach trance to those who cannot achieve it spontaneously; in some societies, such as parts of Bali, trance was expected from all the members of the society at some time in their lives. Since trance is so devalued in our own society, knowledge about it is limited; but it seems probable that some individuals would be incapable of going into trance whatever the climate of opinion and however hard they or their instructors try to produce this physiological response.

The analogy with the female orgasm seems very close. As far as is known, this capacity, like the other cultural options discussed, has no evolutionary significance and has not been reported for any other species of mammal. Several societies have been reported by anthropologists where not even verbal recognition has been given to the possibility of female orgasm but where nevertheless women are deemed to enjoy sexual intercourse as much as, or more than, the men. The demand that all women should achieve orgasm, current in most 'advanced' circles today, would seem to derive, at least in part, from the diffusion of the psychoanalytic ideal of the 'genital character' (female version). Only a statistical study (which is extremely unlikely to be carried out) could determine whether this current version of the 'womanly woman' has increased or decreased feelings of unhappiness and insecurity in the female population affected.

IV

Only in one phrase in the whole of his writings did

Freud acknowledge the possibility that character might be modified by culture; this occurs in his study of a Russian patient, the so-called wolf-man.[29] In the rest of his writings Freud stayed firmly in the tradition of nineteenth-century evolutionism and of the writers of the first decade of the twentieth century who made their massive compendia on aspects of social evolution in their studies. For Freud, as for these writers, the society of which he was a member was self-evidently the culmination of human social evolution; simpler societies, with customs and beliefs sharply contrasting with 'civilization', were survivals representing steps in human evolution which 'civilized' man had passed through and left behind. In this view civilization was a homogeneous concept, and the steps to civilization were arranged in a chronological sequence; tribes who traced their descent through their mothers, for example, were more 'primitive' than those who traced descent through their fathers, regardless of the fact that they were contemporaries; all other criteria, such as technological development or techniques of procuring food, could safely be ignored.*

* An essay could profitably be written on the myths about human evolution and contemporary primitive society current among psychoanalysts. One of the most potent and widespread of these myths is the belief that humanity went through a phase of 'matriarchy' in which the roles of men and women were reversed. No anthropologist today, I think it can be stated with assurance, believes in this construct or any variant of it. Societies vary in the ways in which they trace descent and in the rules for the inheritance of material and immaterial property (such as titles or religious powers); one of these variants, matriliny, traces descent through the mother; property and titles either devolve from mother to daughter, or from brother to sister's son. In such societies the bonds between brother and sister are treated as legally and emotionally more important than the bonds between husband and wife.

In the last years of his life, it would appear, Freud was reproached for paying no attention to the findings of contemporary social anthropologists; in a rather tetchy paragraph in *Moses and Monotheism*,[34] his one from last book, he claims the right to pick the anthropological facts or speculations which are useful to him, and to ignore the rest.

With a few notable exceptions* psychoanalysts have followed Freud's example in paying no attention to the possible modifications which the cultures of different societies might produce in the character-structure of their citizens. This obliviousness to cultural differences is the more remarkable since most of the older psychoanalysts have had the personal experience of migration, of living as adults in more than one society, and in analysing patients from more than one society.

Among the earlier European psychoanalysts, perhaps particularly among those who made the more important theoretical contributions and were most influential as training analysts, there was a high proportion of Jews. As far as is known, all of them were 'assimilated' and few, if any, maintained a belief in Jewish religion or observed the orthodox rituals or dietary taboos; but in the middle-class society of Germany and Austria-Hungary before 1914 they could not escape the negative definition of their nationality ascribed to them by their gentile compatriots. Moreover, though they themselves were emancipated, it is highly likely that many of their families observed orthodox rituals during their formative years; and underlying very many of these rituals (perhaps especially those concerned with food) is an insistence on the unbridgeable difference between the children of

* Chief among these are Géza Róheim[72] and Erik Erikson[11] [12] [15] and their associates and followers.

Israel and the gentiles. Many of these orthodox families had the experience, or the tradition, of moving from one host country to another in the search for less social discrimination and police persecution and maintaining their identity through observing ritual purity and avoiding inter-marriage.

For the emancipated Jews at the turn of the century this orthodox insistence on the separateness and particularity of traditional Jewish culture must have appeared old-fashioned, reactionary and illiberal—all qualities which they repudiated; and therefore any observations they might have made on consistent differences between patients of different cultures or societies had to be repressed or suppressed, lest it give comfort to the reactionaries and, perhaps, call in question the picture of their own identity.* All the emphasis had to be, and was, placed on the psychological unity of the whole of mankind, or at least of all civilized peoples.

Quite inevitably, the early psychoanalysts lived in a predominantly closed group. They were not understood or accepted by the majority of their medical colleagues; and they worked extremely long hours. Psychoanalytic therapy is a very time-consuming process for the analyst; besides treating patients there were notes to be made and papers and books to be written in those extremely productive years. Little wonder that they mostly chose to spend their scant leisure in one another's company.

This pattern of the nearly self-contained group seems to have been established and to have resisted dilution

* An analogous problem faces the liberals and tender-minded today in their relations with peoples of a darker skin-colour. To admit any consistent difference between whites and non-whites would provide ammunition for the racists and other reactionaries.

when psychoanalysis became scientifically more acceptable in the third and fourth decades of this century. It was by then traditional for most psychoanalysts (busier than ever, with a great demand for their services) to spend what leisure they could command in one another's company; their chief relations with the non-psychoanalytic portion of their societies were as spectators or employers.

The migrations following Hitler's seizure of power accentuated this trend. All adult migrants have always had the problems of language, of strange customs and foreign food to make their exile more difficult; even when migration is voluntary, there is a tendency to seek comfort and relaxation among the familiar sounds and tastes and smells. For involuntary migrants a continuation of the pleasures of life *bei uns* may have had even greater attraction.

Moreover, for their skills to be transferable it was obviously desirable to put as little emphasis as could be on the differences between groups of patients and the societies in which they were reared. Exile reinforced the predominance of theory over observation.

The predominance of theory over observation was carried to a logical extreme in the so-called 'British School' of psychoanalysis, deriving from the theory and practice of Mrs Melanie Klein. For Mrs Klein and her followers all the fundamentally significant events in human life occurred in the first months of infancy, well before the acquisition of speech; the only significant relationship with the external world was that of the infant with its mother. Since all the other significant events are assumed to take place in the infant's fantasy, they can never be observed but only reconstructed; and since fantasy is treated as dominant over experience, even if the mother's actual handling of the infant were modified by the customs of the society of which she was a member, this would theoretically be of minor importance. I will discuss later the possible congruence between Mrs Klein's theories and the English view of infantile nature; here I wish to call attention to the theoretical elimination of social variables in a transplanted version of psychoanalysis.

To the best of my knowledge, the only practising psychoanalysts who have made any consistent attempts to take cultural variants into account in a development of psychoanalytic theory are Karen Horney[46] [47] [48] and Erik Erikson,[11] [12] [15] both when they had moved to the United States. I think it is fair to say that both of them have received greater acceptance of their work outside psychoanalytic circles than within them. Karen Horney's later work was rather remote from classical psychoanalysis, for she stressed cultural and situational influences and disregarded the ontogenetic physiological development and vicissitudes of the individual which have always been the corner-stone of Freudian psychoanalytic theory; it is understandable that her influence was not long-lasting. A similar reproach cannot properly be made about Erik Erikson's work.

In some of his later work Jung tended to stress the differences in 'national archetypes'; but these observations were tied to an untenable simplist hypothesis of pseudo-genetics. According to this hypothesis (as far as I can understand it) the archetypes are genetically inherited; but since the populations of all large societies are genetically heterogeneous this explanation is not tenable. The observations may well have some validity; but the theory is capable of being put to base racialist uses.

V

Although the majority of psychoanalysts, as has been shown, have always tended to ignore social and cultural differences, these offer the most probable explanations of the varying acceptance of psychoanalysis, the social status of psychoanalysts and the idiosyncratic theoretical developments in different societies over the last thirty years.

In Britain (I have argued elsewhere)[39] the prevalent view of human development is that children are born with bad and destructive tendencies, an 'animal nature', not knowing right from wrong; and character (implicitly, good character) is formed by the incessant care and watchful attention of parents and guardians to restrain and, if necessary, punish any manifestations of the 'old Adam', the unregenerate animal nature, and to encourage by precept and example self-restraint, discipline and the other characteristics considered peculiarly typical of the 'true' Englishman or Englishwoman.* Any failure to achieve these ideals is considered a reproach to the parents, who are shown to have been insufficiently vigilant; the only palliating excuses are the absence of the parents during the child's formative years (see all the literature on the disastrous effects of the broken home or the working mother) or a 'bad' heredity.

* Confirmation is given by the following quotation from *Patterns of Infant Care in an Urban Community* by J. and E. Newson[70] (page 184) concerning the underlying assumptions of their sample of mothers from Nottingham: "... the theory, sometimes explicitly stated, sometimes merely implied, that early and correct 'habit training' is of considerable importance as a foundation for later character building; and, conversely, that the wrong sort of training in infancy may permanently mar or spoil the child's character."

It would appear to be no accident (to use the Marxist phrase) that the Kleinian version of psychoanalysis has been dubbed the British School. According to Mrs Klein and her followers,[56] [57] infants are filled with the most monstrous murderous and cannibalistic fantasies and wishes; later psychoses are but recapitulations of the 'schizoid' and 'depressive positions' through which all human infants are predestined to pass. There seems to be a close congruence between this construct of the infantile psyche and the less precise beliefs about the 'animal nature' of young children.

It is also probably no accident that it is a British-born psychoanalyst, Dr John Bowlby, who is making the most consistent and imaginative use of the ethologists' observations of animal behaviour to explain and understand the behaviour of infants and young children.[6a, b] To my mind, the revision of the fuzzy psychoanalytic theories of instinct in the light of ethology, on which Dr Bowlby has been engaged for several years, is the most promising development of psychoanalytic theory of recent decades; but as I am a British-born social anthropologist, it is at least theoretically possible that unconscious determinants make these parallels between animal behaviour and the instinctual endowment of the human young particularly convincing.

The British postulate that faults of character in the young are due to parental inadequacy would seem to account for the barely disguised fear that the majority of British parents manifest at the idea of their children having psychoanalytic, or indeed any psychiatric, help. As parents they are (perhaps naturally) unwilling to admit that their offspring are not psychologically as good as possible; and there is the added fear that in the course of the interviews the child or young person may divulge to the psychoanalyst facts about themselves which should be hidden in the bosom of the family, and also that the psychoanalyst may undermine the respect and subvert the moral authority which parents should be accorded. In popular esteem the psychoanalyst (to use the most current generic term for any type of psychiatrist) is a professional spy or snooper, nosing out secrets which you wish to keep hidden. With few exceptions, people tend to be uneasy in his presence; and I doubt whether in Britain psychoanalysts achieve the status or are accorded the esteem granted to surgeons or medical consultants.

"Even before Hitler annexed Austria and drove Freud and his followers into exile," I wrote in *The Americans* in 1947,[38] "the theory and practice of psychoanalysis were more widely spread and widely accepted in the United States than in any other country.... Its diffusion, both directly and in various dilutions, has been very great. Americans have employed the insights derived from psychoanalysis in a number of novel situations, but there have been no major consistent innovations. However, in the process of becoming a naturalized American, as it were, one important aspect of Freud's original theory has been sloughed off, treated as almost nonexistent: all postulates about the inborn wickedness of the child—its aggressive and sadistic 'instincts'—have been abandoned, sometimes by rationalization, sometimes merely by default. In American psychoanalytic thinking, the child is born faultless, a *tabula rasa*, and any defects which subsequently develop are the fault of uncontrollable circumstances, or of the ignorance or malice of its parents who mar what should otherwise be a perfect, or at least perfectly adjusted, human being.... No theory could gain widespread acceptance in America which did not concede that the child was the hope of the future and that he could, given the proper start in life, go further and fare better than his parents."

To the best of my knowledge, this paragraph is still valid. Even though the flow of immigration has dried up to a trickle, the American belief that adults reared in an alien society can be transformed into Americans is still potent; by taking pains and with strength of will one can remake one's personality. This belief has two faces: the positive hope that aliens can become Americans, delinquents can become solid citizens, with help and good will; the negative fear that Americans can be turned into 'communists', loyal citizens into traitors almost without their knowledge by 'brain-washing', by a quasi-magical combination of science and malevolence. Immigrants' children were transformed into hundred per cent Americans with the assistance of teachers, doctors (pediatricians) and often clergymen.

The American psychoanalyst (particularly outside New York and Chicago) seems to have been accorded the status of all these three influential professions: he is perforce a doctor (the number of recognized lay analysts is very small); he is expected to have a moral authority and to point out the road to adjustment like a spiritual guide; and, above all, he is a super-teacher, moulding or re-moulding the character for the more efficient pursuit of happiness, countering those retrograde parental influences which could produce either cultural (for the immigrants' child) or personal (for the analysand) maladjustment.

It is this combination of roles, I believe, which makes a personal psychoanalysis so desirable an addition to the symbols of success for many of the successful in the United States. The psychoanalyst is not merely a medical specialist treating certain symptoms, predominantly psychological; he is also a teacher, a scientific guide to mental health and happiness; everyone who could afford his services would profit by them, as everybody would profit by a university degree.

Everybody who could afford him would profit... the very high cost of a psychoanalytic treatment makes it a patent sign of financial success; and the high fees that the analyst receives show that he is one of the more successful and prominent citizens of the community. In the big cities there are people with few if any qualifications who call themselves psychoanalysts (or a term which looks like it) and provide services at moderate fees for the less prosperous; but the genuine article is a *de luxe* purchase, its value as little questioned as a Cadillac or a yacht.

In the United States a few psychoanalysts (or at least people with some psychoanalytic training) have been willing to use, or hire, their knowledge of unconscious processes for trivial exploitation; unconscious wishes or fears are played upon to increase the sales of minor consumption goods. There is little reason to suppose that this pretentious pseudo-scientific manipulation of unconscious motives is more successful than other more innocent techniques of advertising; but this prostitution of scientific knowledge, even if relatively ineffective, is still deeply distasteful.

In France the theory and practice of psychoanalysis seem to have been almost completely separated. I have no reason to think that psychoanalytic therapy in France differs significantly from that practised elsewhere; but the vocabulary of psychoanalytic theory is used in intellectual and philosophical discourse without any contact, even the most indirect, with psychoanalytic practice. Perhaps the oddest of these writers is Gaston Bachelard, who published a series of musings on the traditional elements, such as fire, with the word 'psychoanalysis' in the title[2]; the texts demonstrate an almost total ignorance of psychoanalysis, apart from a faint recollection of the interpretation of symbols, analogous to that employed by Freud in *Jokes and Their Relation to the Unconscious*[22] or Jung in his later works on alchemy. J.-P. Sartre has used psychoanalysis as if it were a philosophical system, strictly comparable to such philosophic systems as hegelianism or existentialism and equally provable or disprovable by introspection and the employment of coherent, logical and conscious thought; no attention is paid to the fact that the abstractions of psychoanalytic theory are deduced from the observation of the interaction between two people in specified roles.

A number of other intellectuals, less well known outside France, have used the vocabulary in the same fashion, though possibly with less 'brilliance'; the emphasis in the dominant French tradition on the use of systematic logic in civilized intellectual discourse has proved extremely unreceptive to the 'primary process' ascribed by psychoanalysts to the workings and manifestations of the unconscious.

VI

The psychoanalytic ideas which have achieved wide diffusion among educated speakers of English derive almost without exception from the writings of Freud and his associates in the first two decades of this century; the elaboration of ego theory and the analysis of the transference which have marked the more sophisticated writing and practice of the last two decades seem

49

by comparison to have achieved relatively little currency outside the groups of practising analysts and people in contact with them. I think it could be argued, however, that it is these less dramatic theoretical constructs which have the greater potential contribution to the creation of a less unhappy and more rational and efficient society.

In what have practically been pilot studies the insights derived from contemporary psychoanalytic practice and theory have been shown to be useful social tools: in the selection of officers for the forces or the rehabilitation of prisoners of war; in industrial relations, in a very few factories; in the rehabilitation of young delinquent youths at Topeka, Kansas; in a few teacher-training colleges; in even fewer schools. These pilot studies have shown that psychoanalysis can be more than a slow, costly, painful and uncertain technique of therapy; it could, potentially, increase human happiness and efficiency in all institutions where people are in constant interaction. But for this potentiality to become practical, an enormous number of people would have to be trained—teachers, personnel managers, officers and the holders of all positions which entail the control of other people's activities—and, so far, no technique has been evolved for safely imparting these insights except the year-long training analysis. The interpretation of symbols or the recognition of traumata can be learned, after a fashion, from books; the analysis of the transference and counter-transference can, to date, only be learned by experience. Psychoanalysis in the world can make the world a less unhappy place; but this is not going to happen quickly.

The Concept of Cure

ANTHONY STORR

THIS essay will ask more questions than it will attempt to answer; for the idea of cure in psychoanalysis raises fundamental problems in philosophy and ethics of such depth and complexity that the wisest of human beings throughout history have found themselves unable to solve them. That this is so may not be immediately obvious to those who neither practise psychoanalysis nor have, as patients, themselves experienced the process. To the layman, the cure of mental illness may seem analogous to the cure of physical disease. A patient consulting a doctor for a pain in the belly is told that he has appendicitis. An operation is arranged; the diseased appendix removed; and, within a few weeks, the patient finds that he has no pain and is restored to whatever state of health he enjoyed before his appendix became inflamed. A cure has in this instance been effected; and both doctor and patient continue on their respective ways, the former enjoying the satisfaction of having exercised his skill effectively, and the latter appreciating his return to normal health. The less sophisticated patients who consult psychoanalysts not unnaturally expect something similar. If a man suffers from agoraphobia, or from depression, or from homosexuality, he hopes that his symptom will, like an inflamed appendix, be removed from him by psychoanalysis, and that he will then return to a state of mental health in which he can enjoy life once again. In fact, such cures occasionally take place. Most analysts will recall cases in which a single symptom has been quickly abolished in a few psychoanalytic sessions with the result that the patient departs happily, and in which it makes sense to talk of cure. Alexander and French in their book on psychoanalytic therapy give several examples of cases of this kind in which even severe mental symptoms have disappeared after a brief period of treatment.[1] But such cases are the exception rather than the rule. The majority of patients who present themselves for psychoanalysis cannot expect that their symptoms will easily depart or, even if this should happen, that they will then be freed from emotional problems and willing, or able, to discontinue their analytical treatment.

The reason for this is that the majority of symptoms for which persons consult psychoanalysts are not, like a diseased appendix, parts of the patient which he can well be without. Unfortunately, both for patient and analyst, psychoneurotic symptoms are, in most cases, the outward and visible sign of an inner and less visible distortion of the patient's total personality; and the exploration of the symptoms inevitably leads on to a consideration of the whole person, his development, temperament, and character structure.

Suppose, for example, that a man consults an analyst for impotence. This distressing and humiliating symptom may be a temporary phenomenon which is easily relieved in a very short time. Many men hold the belief that they ought to be potent under all circumstances, and become distressed and anxious when they are not. If an unmarried man of thirty-five is having an affair with a married woman, and the only place available for love-making is the back of a car, he can hardly expect to be as potent as he would be in the privacy and comfort of his own familiar bedroom. For love to find its fullest physical expression, spontaneity and ease are essential; and no one can be spontaneous and relaxed when feeling guilty and physically uncomfortable. The type of impotence which occurs under circumstances of this kind may be quickly relieved after a short period of psychotherapy with the result that the patient goes away cured. On the other hand, impotence may be, and often is, the only obvious symptom of a profound disorder of personality in which the whole of the patient's life is inhibited or distorted, and may thus be either difficult or impossible to cure.

Moreover, even in cases where the symptom is rapidly removed, its investigation is apt to raise such far-reaching questions of the patient's whole personality that both patient and analyst will want to pursue matters further. In the example given above, for instance, all kinds of questions spring to mind which lead far beyond the immediate problem of the patient's impotence. Why, for example, does he expect to be fully potent under such adverse circumstances? Is he carrying on into adult life an infantile fantasy of being omnipotent?

Why is he having an affair with a married woman, whom he can only see with difficulty? Is it that he is playing safe, frightened of committing himself to a more complete relation; and if so, what are the fears of women which he harbours and how did they originate? At the age of thirty-five, most men are married. What has prevented this particular man from becoming so? Has he some persistent emotional entanglement with parents or siblings from which he has been unable to free himself, or is he bisexual, with a partial or predominant libidinal attachment to men?

It is not difficult to see that, even if the symptom of impotence is quickly relieved, the questions inevitably raised by the symptom may lead to a full psychoanalytic exploration of the patient's total personality. Moreover, this exploration is not one foisted upon an unwilling patient by a rapacious analyst; at least, certainly not in this country, where the demand for analysis greatly exceeds its availability. In very many instances, patients rapidly lose interest in the symptoms for which they originally sought treatment, whether or not these symptoms are actually relieved; and the process of analysis becomes an end in itself, a journey of exploration which is undertaken for its own sake; not so much a treatment, more a way of life.

It is probable, that, in the near future, the distinction between removal of symptoms and psychoanalysis will become more sharply defined. The advent of methods of treatment based upon learning theory and conditioning should be welcomed by analysts, for the questions raised by these methods will help analysts to clarify their own minds as to what it is they actually do. These methods, which can be subsumed under the general heading of 'behaviour therapy', attack neurotic symptoms direct and are sometimes successful in eliminating them. The behaviour therapist shows no interest in the origin of the symptom, nor in the patient's personality as a whole. He is concerned only with the abolition of the symptom, and makes no attempt to explore the patient's world of unconscious fantasy even if he admits the existence of such a phenomenon. At the time of writing, the methods of the behaviour therapists are too recent for a full assessment of their results. There can be no doubt, however, that they are successful in abolishing certain kinds of symptoms in some cases. When discussing impotence at the beginning of this essay, a tentative distinction was made between symptoms which inevitably lead to a full exploration of the patient's total personality and those which do not. It is with the latter group of symptoms that the behaviour therapists are particularly successful.

Some phobias, for example, persist as habits long after the emotional conflict or trauma which gave origin to them, has disappeared. One case, for example, was that of a professional man who suffered from an intense fear of thunderstorms. Since thunderstorms are not uncommon in Britain, he was often in a state of considerable tension, fearing that he would incur the ridicule of his colleagues if he suddenly felt obliged to seek refuge from thunder by hiding under a table or retiring to a lavatory. His symptom took origin from a traumatic experience in early childhood in which he had nearly been struck by a flash of lightning which was accompanied by a deafening clap of thunder. In other respects, a more or less superficial enquiry indicated that this man was both happy and successful. This isolated phobia of thunderstorms had little obvious connection with the rest of his character structure; but, like a diseased appendix, was a pathological appendage of which he would have been thankful to be rid, and the removal of which was likely to cause small disturbance to the rest of his personality. In such a case, a behaviour therapist would probably expose the patient gradually to increasing intensities of the noise of thunder and electrical flashes; at first, perhaps, combining this with sedation or other methods of extinguishing responses. When the patient had become sufficiently accustomed to reacting without fear to artificial thunder and lightning in the laboratory, it would be hoped that he could finally be exposed to a real thunderstorm and discover that his response of fear had been abolished.

If behaviour therapy had been available at the time that this patient was seen, the author would undoubtedly have advised it : but such cases, unfortunately, are the exception rather than the rule in psychiatric practice. The majority of phobias do not spring from isolated traumatic incidents, but are intimately connected with the patient's style of life and his whole development from childhood onwards.

The common symptom of agoraphobia, for example, is usually linked with the persistence of childhood dependency, fear of abandonment by the mother, and also with fears of the patient's own sexuality and aggression. The presenting symptom of being frightened to cross an open space or street unaccompanied is only the peak of the iceberg. This symptom often occurs in girls of twenty or so whose emotional development has been retarded. Enquiry generally reveals that such a girl is not only frightened of open spaces, but cannot do her own shopping, cannot be left in the house alone, and is fearful of making any independent move without the approval and support of her mother. In other words, she shows behaviour which would be expected in a child of four or five, but which is inappropriate to her chronological age of twenty. Accompanying her overt fears of being left alone without support, it will regularly be discovered that she is frightened of any instinctual response which might incur parental disapproval. Her fear of crossing the street alone will often be associated with fears both that men will make sexual advances to her, and also that she will respond to such approaches. It will also be discovered that she is fearful of her own aggressive feelings towards her mother. If, at an earlier stage in her development, she had been able to display that normal degree of self-assertiveness which is essential if children are to reach independence, she would have learned to be more self-reliant. In such cases, however, it is generally discovered that the mother has both discouraged a show of active rebellion against her authority, and has also over-protected the child by habitually doing for her innumerable daily tasks which she should have learned to carry out for herself.

From this abbreviated account it must be obvious that the study of a single phobia may, and often should, lead to a consideration of the patient's whole personality and relations with other people; and that abolition of the single symptom of agoraphobia, even if this were possible, would not relieve the patient of the bulk of her emotional problems. The same is true of by far the majority of neurotic symptoms.

It might, therefore, be concluded that the problem of neurosis was a simple one. Those people who present with symptoms, which, like the phobia of thunderstorms, are superficial excrescences on the surface of a basically healthy personality can be safely turned over to the behaviour therapist with the prospect of fairly rapid alleviation. The others, whose symptoms are obviously part and parcel of their character structure, must be referred for psychoanalysis in the hope that this far-ranging and deep exploration will relieve their symptoms by a reorganization of their total personality, thus bringing about a cure.

Unfortunately, the problem is not so simple as it might appear. On the practical level, psychoanalysis is so expensive and time-consuming that relatively few persons can afford it. Nor, in England or the U.S.A., are there nearly enough analysts available to undertake the analysis of the patients who demand it or are referred for it. Any psychiatrist who is himself analytically trained or habitually sends patients to psychoanalysts knows that to find an analyst with a vacancy for treatment is often extremely difficult. The demand for psychoanalysis greatly exceeds its availability; and, in the U.S.A., where psychoanalysis is more generally accepted than in England, a variant of Parkinson's Law is operative, so that the more trained analysts become available, the more patients seek out their professional services. This is the more remarkable, since the evidence that psychoanalysis cures anybody of anything is so shaky as to be practically non-existent.

During the past fifteen years, Professor Eysenck and other opponents of psychoanalysis have repeatedly asserted, with some justice, that such statistics as exist do not support the hypothesis that psychoanalysis is an effective treatment for neurosis. Comparative studies have been made in which a group of neurotic persons treated by psychoanalysis have been compared with some similar groups, either treated by different methods or not treated at all. The recovery rate in each group has been shown to be similar, although, according to

Eysenck, the group treated by psychoanalysis shows a wider variability of outcome, in that it contains both a greater number of patients who recover and also a greater number who get worse.[17] The American Psychoanalytic Association, who might be supposed to be prejudiced in favour of their own speciality, undertook a survey to test the efficacy of psychoanalysis. The results obtained were so disappointing that they were withheld from publication.[64]

In practice, however, most psychoanalysts consider it their professional duty *not* to make any promise of cure to their patients. This is partly because they are anxious not to give reassurance, a technique which may give temporary encouragement but which seldom solves, and may obscure, the patient's problems. It is also because the results of the psychoanalytic process are genuinely unpredictable. The more experienced an analyst is, the more does he realize that cases which initially seem to promise rapid resolution prove long and difficult, whereas others, apparently more deeply disturbed, turn out to be relatively simple problems. In attempting to assess the efficacy of psychoanalysis as a method of treatment, both critics and supporters have concentrated on the question of whether or not this approach actually relieves neurotic symptoms. Indeed, what else could they do? Yet, in practice, both analysts and patients know that, once the analysis is under way, the question of the relief of symptoms tends to become less and less relevant. It is not uncommon to hear analysts say with relief about a patient that he has passed the stage of bothering with symptoms at all, irrespective of whether they have disappeared or not, and this lack of concern with symptoms is reckoned as a sign of progress in analysis. In other words, most analyses which go on for any length of time tend to become something which can no longer be designated as treatment at all; a fact which led a cynical critic to say that psychoanalysis becomes itself the disease of which the patient seeks to be cured.

The fact that the relief of symptoms so often becomes a partially irrelevant issue is also because the majority of patients who now present themselves for analysis do not have any clear-cut symptoms in any case. In analytical practice, it is now rare to encounter a patient who falls into any of the diagnostic categories which can be found in textbooks of psychiatry. Most patients show a mixture of obsessional, hysterical, depressive and schizoid traits; and seek analysis because their lives are unhappy and their personal relationships disturbed and unrewarding. Thus, a representative analytical practice might perhaps contain a minister of religion with doubts about his faith, a woman whose husband has left her for another, a male homosexual complaining of depression and isolation, a psychiatric social worker with emotional difficulties in dealing with her clients, a business man with a duodenal ulcer, a composer whose inspiration has deserted him, and a mother whose chief complain is of an inability to handle the upbringing of her children.

All these people might well exhibit a variety of neurotic symptoms; but the reason that each sought analysis would be that their lives had become so unhappy that they felt obliged to look for help. Jung once said that analysis was for people "at the end of their tether", and although this statement cannot fully be supported, since doctors and others seek analysis for professional reasons when not in a state of great emotional distress, there is a good deal of truth in Jung's remark.

Moreover, it is a commonplace observation that we

all have neurotic symptoms. As a colleague once said to me: "The normal man is a very dark horse indeed." The better one gets to know both one's friends and oneself, the more can one see in operation the identical defence mechanisms, neurotic character traits and periodic symptoms which are presented in the course of analysis by a patient on the couch. In other words, patients can only be distinguished from non-patients by the fact that they present themselves for analysis, and not because they are noticeably more neurotic than those who do not seek an analyst's assistance. In the hypothetical group of patients which we designated above, the analyst is confronted with unhappy people who may be desperate about their emotional problems; but no one thinks of unhappiness or even desperation as being necessarily neurotic symptoms. The factors which determine whether unhappy people seek analytical help or not have very little to do with the kind of symptoms or emotional problems which trouble them. Whether the patient has ever heard of analysis, whether he can afford it, and whether an analyst is available to him, are all more likely to be determinants of his course of action than are his symptoms or emotional dilemmas.

It follows from what has been said that psychoanalysts are habitually dealing with a clientèle which is highly selected, very varied, and which is not necessarily ill in any definable sense. This clientèle cannot easily be distinguished from so-called normals, who happen to be going through periods of emotional stress. This being so, it becomes even more dubious to talk of cure in psychoanalysis; for, as one critic has put it, "If one is not entirely sure that a patient is sick before treatment, how can he be judged to be well after it?"

This difficulty can, I believe, be resolved, if we cease

to regard psychoanalysis as a treatment comparable to medical or surgical treatment, and can also school ourselves to think of cure in psychological problems as a relative, rather than an absolute, term. If it is accepted that psychoanalysis is not primarily a method of treatment for neurotic symptoms, it becomes relevant to ask what on earth it is. This question has been answered by Dr Rycroft in his Introduction on 'Causes and Meaning', in which he advances the hypothesis that psychoanalysis is a semantic theory of which the main function is that of making sense out of the verbal communications which the patient offers. This conclusion itself makes sense out of psychoanalysis; although it must be understood that the process of interpreting what the patient says is not simply an intellectual exercise, but involves the consideration and evocation of the most powerful emotions which human beings experience. There remains the question of whether the increased understanding of himself in terms of psychoanalytic theory which a patient may gain is actually of any value. In other words, has psychoanalysis any curative or healing effect whatever?

I believe that it has, but that the idea of cure in psychoanalysis is analogous to the cure of physical disease ought to be finally discarded. Dr Rycroft pointed out in his preface that the relief of symptoms depended upon other factors than the patient's understanding of them; upon the attitude of those close to the patient, his own conscious ideals, religious beliefs and so on. This being so, it becomes easier to comprehend the paradox which must have puzzled many analysts and some patients. I refer to the fact that a good many people continue to seek psychoanalytic assistance even when their symptoms have been both understood and relieved.

There are also a number of patients whose immediate symptoms are not relieved, but who nevertheless want to continue with analysis because they have found something valuable in the process. This value, it will be argued, is not necessarily analogous to cure as that word is ordinarily used.

There can be little doubt that there is some confusion amongst analysts themselves about the healing effect of their technique, for they use a wide variety of terms to describe their concepts of health and the prerequisites for obtaining this blissful condition. When Freud first discovered the 'talking cure', he found that the recollection of painful incidents in the patient's childhood produced relief in some cases. This led analysts to suppose that the uncovering of buried traumata was the main objective of the analytic process. An elderly psychoanalyst, for example, was once discussing the case of a man who had been in analysis for many years. From a study of dreams and other material, the analyst was convinced that, in very early childhood, his patient had been the subject of a homosexual assault. If only, he averred, the man could recall this incident, together with the emotion which accompanied it, there could be no doubt of his final recovery. This naïve point of view is no longer held by the majority of analysts, and was indeed abandoned by Freud quite early in his career. Traumatic incidents are undoubtedly important, as in the case of the man with a phobia of thunderstorms which was quoted earlier: but their significance is more generally that of throwing light upon the emotional climate in which the patient was reared rather than that of being isolated causes of later neurosis. Being shut in a cupboard at the age of three may have induced stress at the time; but being unfortunate enough to have parents who considered that this was an appropriate way of dealing with a naughty child is a more likely cause of later maladjustment. Nor is it possible to maintain that the recovery of the emotions connected with such incidents is in itself a major factor in healing. Abreaction, the explosive expression of powerful emotions of love, hate or fear, may cure certain cases of traumatic neurosis. Indeed, most of us feel better for giving vent to emotions which we have had to control, or by which we are alarmed, and acknowledgement and expression of emotion is certainly one valuable feature of the psychoanalytic process. Every analyst, however, will have had patients who continue for long periods to express violent emotion at every session, but who do not show improvement as a result.

No one doubts that insight is a valuable acquisition. The Socratic injunction to know oneself was accepted by reflective men centuries before Freud was ever heard of. Nor is it possible to dispute that psychoanalysis does bring insight. Even if the analyst were to make no interpretation or comment at all, the patient would be bound to gain some increase in the understanding of his own mental processes; for no one can talk about himself for hour after hour without augmenting his self-knowledge. The patient who uttered the classic remark "I don't know what I think until I hear what I say," expressed an important truth about the human condition, and even those who reject the whole of psychoanalytic theory must needs admit that the expression in words of what one thinks and feels is itself a clarification of those thoughts and feelings.

Insight has long been an analytical battle-cry. Those who possess it or attain it are the sheep; the rest, who live their lives in simplicity and ignorance, are the goats.

But it remains uncertain as to how far insight either relieves distress or modifies behaviour. Jung tells the story of a young man who came to him with a complete case history of his own neurosis. So far as Jung could ascertain, the historical reconstruction of his disorder was complete, his understanding of his own condition unassailable. In spite of his insight, he was not cured; and his behaviour towards other people indicated that his human relationships were far from being either admirable or satisfying. Most psychoanalysts would say that such a person possessed intellectual insight only; and would contrast the limited gains thus obtained with the richer benefits accruing from what is termed emotional or affective insight. But even if the patient's reconstruction had been accompanied by every emotion in the gamut, it is safe to say that he might have still been neurotic. Insight, as many analysts have themselves discovered, is not enough; unless the term is misused, as it often is, to imply that it is equivalent to healing.

During the past forty years innumerable concepts of psychological health have been advanced. Psychoanalysis, although propounding a complicated hypothetical structure of the mental apparatus in psychological terms, has always recognized that man's emotional experience is rooted in the body, and that it is emotion which gives meaning to life. The Freudian scheme of the development of infantile sexuality postulates a beginning in the infant's relation to the breast. The end, which we all hope to attain, is termed full genitality. That is, the ability to have a full relation with the opposite sex in which the genitals play the major part in obtaining satisfaction is a touchstone of health; and cure consists in the attainment of full genitality by a patient who, until he was analysed, had not been able to arrive at this blessed state. Those unfamiliar with psychoanalytic terminology may suppose that full genitality is but a modest goal which most of us could expect to achieve without too much difficulty. After all, nature is on one's side; and it should not be beyond the capability of psychoanalysts so to relieve feelings of sexual inferiority and guilt that many of their patients could succeed in making full use of their genital potential. Unfortunately, this is not what psychoanalysts mean.

There is a sense in which full genitality does represent an end-point in human emotional development; and it is perfectly right to suppose that neurotic persons have, in most instances, failed to reach this end-point. But an examination of what psychoanalysts imply by this concept reveals that the term is an abbreviation for an ideal state of health which extends to include every aspect both of the patient's own emotional life and also of his relations with other people. Thus, a Don Juan who was successful with women would certainly not be considered to have achieved full genitality, but to have remained in the narcissistic phase of development; for the term refers not only to the ability to have intercourse, but also to a man's total relation with a woman.

There are many variants upon the same theme. The apparently modest goal turns out to be an abstract ideal of perfection. Another way of expressing the same idea is to say that human beings ought to be capable of mature object relationships, and that this is the acid test of psychic health. A mature object relationship is one in which the patient has overcome his infantile dependency and his emotional attachment to his parents and siblings, and been able to make satisfying relationships with other people in which neither identification nor projection play an important part. Fully to explore the concept of mature object relations would require at least one complete book. Here, it must suffice to make the dogmatic statement that this idea actually comprises so much that it too is a shorthand term for an ideal state of psychological health in which the patient is either supposed to have no emotional problems, or else to be able to solve any that arise with complete assurance.

The same is true of various other concepts of mental well-being. 'Emotional maturity' is a goal which, the nearer one approaches to it recedes the faster; and so is 'integration'. 'Self-realization' and 'self-actualization' are invariably aims rather than actual achievements. The search for identity is a never-ending quest; whilst the attempt to distinguish the true from the false self may be an equally interminable endeavour.

Psychoanalysis and its derivatives have often been criticized for aiming at an ideal state of mental health which no human being ever in fact achieves. It has been asserted that analyses of many years' duration go on for so long because the analyst is obsessed with his Utopian goal and will not rest content until his patient has achieved it. Whilst this accusation is not generally true, since most analysts and most patients are satisfied with more modest achievements, the fact that there are ideals of the kind mentioned above throws light on some of the current confusion about the idea of cure.

The notion that the cure of symptoms alone is the function of psychoanalysis has already been dismissed. When, however, we come to examine the exploration of the whole personality with which most analyses are now concerned, we are inevitably faced with the fact that no patient can ever be completely cured, since no one can reach the ideal state of maturity, integration,

or whatever one likes to name it, which is invariably
called in question the moment any analysis proceeds
beyond the point of dealing with immediate symptoms.
It is this fact which, in the first sentence of this essay,
led me to state that the idea of cure in psychoanalysis
raised fundamental problems of philosophy. For, if a
patient is drawn by his disturbed state of mind to examine the whole of his personality, he is bound to come
up against such questions as: What constitutes human
happiness? How far ought one to pursue one's own
happiness if this involves the unhappiness of others?
How far does a person exist in the absence of relations
with other persons? And even: What is the meaning of
life, or has it any meaning at all?

Analysts may maintain with justice that they are no
better fitted than the next man to answer philosophical
problems which have puzzled the wisest of men since
thought began, although many of them fail to display
the modesty which ought to become them. Nevertheless,
they cannot escape the responsibility of defining their
own position, since what they believe about the nature
of man will influence what they say to the patient, and
the kind of interpretation which they place on what
their patient says to them. It is clear that, however de-
tached and objective a psychoanalyst may try to be, he
cannot entirely escape his own preconceptions; and
these will influence his patient whether he wants them
to or not, for his preconceptions will determine the
relative value he places upon his patient's different
utterances, and this is bound to communicate itself.

Dr Rycroft, in his Introduction, outlined this problem
very precisely without going into an elaboration in
detail. After suggesting that psychoanalysis is a semantic
theory, he goes on to suggest that analysts should con-

centrate "on improving their technique for getting into communication with those who have become alienated for whatever reason". According to Dr Rycroft, therefore, those who seek analysis are alienated; and their cure presumably consists in abolishing or reducing their alienation. (The word 'alienation' has become fashionable on account of its use by existentialists. Its use by others does not imply acceptance of the whole of the existentialist point of view.) Dr Rycroft goes on to describe the self as "a psychobiological entity which is always striving for self-realization and self-fulfilment", and assumes that there is an impersonal force within human beings from which in illness they become in some sense separated. These, in fact, are Dr Rycroft's basic preconceptions about the nature of man; and, unlike most analysts, he is explicit in stating them. He goes on to assert that psychoanalysis is a biological theory of meaning. What is implied by these statements is first, that man shares with other animals the same basic drives; and second, that it is alienation from 'the impersonal force within' which is responsible for the kind of disorder which brings them to the psychoanalyst. The analyst's task, therefore, is that of interpreting the patient's verbal utterances and behaviour in such a way that they are recurrently related to the primitive, biological drives which we share with the animal kingdom; in the hope that, by being once more put in touch with his basic inner nature, the patient will be able to discover better ways of expressing this in actual living.

In this view of psychoanalysis, therefore, health consists in being in touch with instinct, and cure in overcoming the alienation from instinct which particularly afflicts human beings because of their complexity and plasticity. The analyst's task is so to interpret what the patient offers him that the latter is recurrently reintroduced to his own instinctive roots. This way of regarding cure by psychoanalysis has the merit that it removes the all-or-none element which, to some people seems implicit in the word. For it is clear that a person can be more o. less alienated from instinct, and therefore can be more or less cured by psychoanalysis. Although, presumably, there must be an ideal state of non-alienation, the very fact that this has to be expressed by a negative divests it of the idealistic overtones which reverberate around phrases such as 'emotional maturity'. However, there are also objections to this way of regarding cure in psychoanalysis.

The first is that there is still disagreement as to what constitutes the instinctive equipment of man. If neurotic unhappiness is the result of alienation from instinct, and psychoanalysis a method of putting a man in touch with his instincts, it ought surely to be agreed as to what these instincts are. However, biologists are still uncertain both as to the number of the primary instincts in man and other animals, and even as to the nature of instinct itself. Instinct may be defined as an inborn, innate impulse to seek a particular satisfaction; a drive which arises internally, and which creates stress or discomfort in the animal until it is expressed in action. Many biologists believe that there are five primary instincts: reproduction, nutrition, social relations, sleep, and care of the body surface. Others would add aggression: and whether or no there is actually an aggressive instinct is still a subject of controversy, in biology as much as in psychology and psychoanalysis. Until we know from research more about man's fundamental instinctive requirements, we may expect that there will continue to be theoretical disagreements between psychoanalysts. Fortunately, direct observation of infants and experimental work with our nearest animal relatives, the other primates, is already illuminating the problem; and it may confidently be expected that, within the next fifty years, the ethological approach to human behaviour will throw considerable light upon the instinctive equipment of man, the basic needs of infants and children, and upon what harmful consequences can be expected when these needs are not met. We already know that, in other species, conditions analogous to schizophrenia can be produced by isolation. We also know that homosexuality and other disorders of instinct can be determined and made permanent in animals by manipulation of the environment. One of the strongest arguments in favour of psychoanalysis is that it considers man as a biological phenomenon. One of the weakest points in its theoretical structure, is that we know so little of man from just this point of view. Ethological research is, however, tending to confirm some psychoanalytic hypotheses; and, in time, it seems likely that we shall possess a theory of human development and instinct to which most analysts will be able to subscribe. [4] [65] [82] [87] A second objection to regarding cure in psychoanalysis as the result of overcoming alienation from instinct is the fact that neurotic distress can be, and often is, ameliorated by methods in which consideration of instinct plays no part. Eysenck and other critics postulate a spontaneous recovery rate of a high order, and it is possible that they may be right, since a person's emotional state and attendant circumstances are bound to vary, with the result that a good many people will certainly feel better within a year or two of the onset of their troubles, without the intervention of a psychoanalyst. Nevertheless, it has never really been demonstrated that these recoveries are

as spontaneous as they appear. Without the most detailed investigation, how is one to know that many of the
patients did not in fact come into contact with influences of various kinds which helped them, and which
did for them at least some part of what an analyst would
try to do? A research programme designed to investigate
all the factors which contribute to recovery would be
of more value than one which simply tries to demonstrate that psychoanalysis is ineffective.

It seems probable that there are two main factors
which promote a person's recovery from the kind of
neurotic distress which we have been considering. Both
enter into psychoanalysis but neither are peculiar to it;
and each factor may operate independently upon
patients who are not being analysed but seeking help
in other ways. The first factor is that the patient adopts
some scheme or system of thought which appears to him
to make sense out of his distress. The second is that he
makes a relationship of a fruitful kind with another
person.

The need to make sense out of neurotic suffering is
an interesting aspect of human psychology. When a
man is tortured by depression, or guilt, or by sexual
or aggressive impulses which he finds difficult to accept
or control, any explanation of his difficulties, however
partial, will bring some sense of relief. Thus, even such
platitudes as "Man is born to suffering as the sparks fly
upwards" at least carry the implication that conflict is
only to be expected as part of human existence and that
he is therefore not singular in his distress. More elabor-
ate schemata which either explain symptoms, or else
relate human suffering to some cosmic system or *Welt-
anschauung* bring more substantial relief. Many people
can be persuaded, for example, that the fault lies not in

themselves but in their stars. An unfortunate conjunction of the planets at the time of their birth is responsible for their symptoms; and astrological guidance based upon the horoscope will help them to overcome their difficulties. Others take comfort from theosophy, from spiritualism, and from various even more bizarre systems which bring both explanation and reassurance. The depression which follows bereavement has, for example, often induced a person to seek out a medium who will obtain messages from the spirit of the deceased; and, if the communications prove convincing, the unhappy person will both find that his depression is alleviated and also be likely to adopt a system of belief about another existence to follow which is some compensation for his dissatisfaction with his present life on earth.

Such beliefs are, of course, more satisfying when they are shared by others; but this is not an essential part of their therapeutic effect. One patient who, during her twenties, remained in bed for seven years on account of hysterical symptoms, was told by her mother that her illness was a sign of especial favour by the Deity, who was evidently reserving her for some great work as yet unspecified. This brought her comfort for a while, since it gave some meaning to her illness, although it tended to make her symptoms persist instead of relieving them, since to rise from her bed would have been to flout the Deity.

The most private and bizarre beliefs are the delusional systems of schizophrenic patients, which, in spite of their essentially personal origin, resemble each other so closely that they attest the basic similarity of human nature, and, more especially, man's need for explanatory systems. A paranoid person who believes that his aggressive and sexual thoughts are not his own, but are

73

introduced into his mind by the evil machinations of others, and that his lack of success in life is the result of a widespread conspiracy, is adopting a system of thought which both preserves his self-esteem and absolves him from the necessity of acknowledging the reality of his own instincts. Such a delusional system may not work very well, especially if the patient can find no one to share it; but it does protect him from total despair and disintegration; and this accounts for the fact that delusional beliefs are so resistant to therapeutic interpretation.

The need to make sense out of suffering has evidently inspired a good deal of religious and philosophical thinking. Depression, for example, has been explained as an affliction by the devil, as punishment for sin, or as a dark night of the soul which the sufferer must endure in order to be reunited with the Deity : whilst life itself has been regarded as a vale of tears through which human beings have perforce to pass before they can attain the joys of paradise. The human hunger for finding some explanation for suffering is, of course, only a special instance for the need to make sense out of existence itself which underlies not only religion and philosophy, but also science. Man is a very small creature in a vast and largely uncomprehended universe. Any system which relates parts to a whole, and creates order out of chaos, has an immediate appeal; for, even if comprehension does not necessarily confer the power to influence events, it at least grants some security by seeming to inform a man what are the facts of existence to which he has to adapt himself. Thus, knowledge of the law of gravitation does not enable man to modify the courses of the planets; but it does enable predictions to be made about the future of the earth which are reassuring, and relates our own planet to others in a manner which makes sense, thus diminishing the primitive fear that Nature may be arbitrary or capricious.

Similarly, explanations of human nature which make neurotic symptoms comprehensible may not in fact enable people to get rid of their symptoms; but they do provide relief because of our fear of chaos, especially if this seems to be within us. It is partly on this account that patients in analysis claim to be receiving benefit even if their symptoms are not improved. Nor is this because, as is sometimes supposed, the patient is relieved from responsibility by being enabled to blame his disorder upon parents or other people. Psychoanalysis may certainly give explanations in terms of the failure of early environment to meet the patient's needs. Emancipation from the effects of such failure, however, which is one aim of analysis, makes the patient more responsible for himself, not less. Discovering who one is, and how one came to be as one is, increases the sense of personal responsibility since one becomes less helplessly at the mercy of the emotional influences of the past, and thereby gains a wider choice of action.

Since any explanatory scheme, however absurd, may bring a patient some relief, it is legitimate and indeed necessary to ask whether the psychoanalytic interpretation of human behaviour has any claim to be considered closer to the truth than any other.

'To every man his own delusional system' is a likely principle of human existence; and the evidence that psychoanalysis is more than yet another delusional system is slender. Nevertheless, psychoanalysis is the only way of regarding human behaviour which, to date, possesses the twin advantages of doing justice to man's complexity, and, at the same time, relating this complexity to the biological characteristics which make him part of Nature. As such, it must continue to promote both speculation and research; which is as much as ought to be asked of any theory of human behaviour.

It was suggested above that the second main factor which promotes a person's recovery from neurotic suffering is the formation of a fruitful relationship with another person. We all, when emotionally distressed, turn to other people for help, unless we suffer from the almost total emotional isolation which afflicts the schizophrenic. None of us exists alone; for man is a social being, and the very concept of individuality or personality depends upon interrelationship. As John Macmurray[66] puts it: "The personal relation of persons is constitutive of personal existence: there can be no man until there are at least two men in communication." It follows that a man who is alienated from himself is inevitably alienated from others; and the restoration of contact with his own instinctive roots goes hand-in-hand with, and is indeed the same process as, the restoration of personal relationships.

It is clear that a person in distress who turns to another is likely to obtain some kind of help. Whether he approaches a relative, a friend, a priest, or even the correspondence column of a weekly journal, he will be given sympathy, counsel, and at least a modicum of understanding: and this may bring him some relief in his predicament. In fact, profound emotional upheavals often lead to an increased depth of relationship with another person, for the sufferer is forced by his distress to confide and to trust in a way which he may never have been able to do before, and this in itself may heal the division within him. It is probable that many of the so-called spontaneous cures of neurosis in fact occur in

76

this manner; though research would be required to prove this.

Nevertheless, the kind of help which a distressed person may obtain in this way is subject to severe limitations. The world is full of kindly and generous people who are willing to extend sympathy and compassion; but they are usually prone to accompany this with a great deal of good advice, since few can resist the temptation of telling others what to do in the human predicaments which afflict us all. Jung once wrote: "Good advice is often a doubtful remedy, but generally not dangerous since it has so little effect." This statement is right so far as it goes, but leaves out of account the effect which the attitude underlying the giving of advice or repeated reassurance is likely to have on the person who receives it. Analysts give as little advice and reassurance as they can, because to do so actually interferes with the patient's recovery. It is ultimately denigrating to another person to instruct him how to live or simply to bolster him up. We are all human beings faced with the same human problems, carrying the burden of our humanity. Analysts know no better than anyone else how a particular life should be lived; but may justly claim that what they do know is how to increase a person's understanding of himself, and thus enable him to make decisions concerning his life which are more in accordance with his actual nature. It is always easier to subscribe to charity than it is to find ways of enabling the poverty-stricken to overcome their own problems: but implicit in the practice of handing out bounty is the assumption that the recipient is an inferior who cannot make a living for himself.

It is because of this that analysts, unlike other helpers, try as far as possible to keep their own opinions and personalities out of the situation; and, although no one can do this completely, the fact that the analyst obtrudes himself so little is one feature of the analytical approach to human problems which renders it unique. If we are right in postulating that the formation of a fruitful relation with another person is a potent factor in healing, it may be argued that the analyst's detachment and refusal to reveal himself is actually inimical to the patient forming such a relation. It is a truism to assert that neurotic difficulties spring from emotional deprivation in childhood; and it has often been affirmed, even by analysts themselves, that it is love which really heals the patient. This being so, it is arguable that what is needed is not understanding on the part of the patient, but love on the part of the analyst. Would not a conventional Good Samaritan approach be as effective, or more effective, than a technique in which the analyst simply interprets?

The answer to this is simple, though singularly unappreciated. Analysis cannot be a therapy of replacement, nor is it desirable that it should be so. No analyst can make up for a rejecting mother or an absent father, nor can he be a lover, however ardently his patient may wish it. Implicit in the analytical relation is the idea that the analyst is a reliable, consistent person who will remain more or less the same during the patient's contact with him. But he cannot and should not offer love direct. Rather is he a kind of sounding-board against which the patient can test out the nature of his alienation from other people, which, as we have said, goes hand in hand with his alienation from himself.

Many analysts believe, with reason, that analysis of the so-called transference is the keystone of the analytical process. As indicated above, this cannot be regarded as the whole story; but it is certainly true that it is one of the two major factors in promoting recovery. An alienated person is so because through fear, guilt, self-abasement or suspicion he is unable to communicate freely with others. He cannot reveal his true self to another human being because he does not believe that any other human being can accept him as he actually is. It is here that the technique of psychoanalysis plays so important a role.

The technique of psychoanalysis requires that the analyst seldom gives advice or direct reassurance, as we have said above. Instead, the analyst listens carefully to what is presented to him, and tries first to disentangle and then to interpret the underlying emotional threads which form the warp and woof of the patient's discourse. In this way, he tries to re-establish connections which have been lost; the links between the patient's overt utterances and the instinctive roots which, psychoanalysts believe, are the prime movers of human conduct. If these connections can be re-established, the patient will not need to ask what he should do next or how he should behave; for he will know, from the depths of his own being, what the pattern of his life must be.

This internal process of reconnecting with instinct is, however, repeatedly blocked or inhibited by the patient's failure to allow himself to talk freely in the presence of the analyst. People only reveal their most intimate feelings to another person if they can trust that person; that is, if no doubts, suspicions, or fears intervene between themselves and the person in whom they are attempting to confide. In terms of the definition of neurosis which was put forward above, however, it is just because doubts, fears and suspicions have alienated the patient

79

both from other people and himself that he finds himself in an emotional predicament. If he had been able, in the past, to trust his own feelings and to trust other people with them, he would not have become neurotically disturbed. When, therefore, he confronts the analyst, he inevitably tends to treat him as he has treated others in the past; as someone in whom he cannot freely confide for fear of scorn or rejection. It is the way of handling these particular phenomena which is peculiar to analysis; and which gives it a claim to be considered superior to other methods for aiding those in emotional distress.

By keeping his own personality in the background, and revealing as little of himself as possible, the analyst presents the patient with an enigma. The less the patient knows, the more will his picture of the analyst be coloured by his experience of people in the past; and the clearer will be the analyst's and the patient's perception of what has gone amiss with his previous human relationships. By being, so far as he can, no more than a reliable, unknown person, the analyst makes it possible for the patient to see in him a variety of persons and possibilities. An ink-blot is more evocative of subjective preconception than a skilful portrait; a blank sheet of paper than a column of newsprint; and so the analyst's refusal to impose his own personality evokes from the patient guesses, hopes, fears and suspicions which would not manifest themselves if the analyst was a known and definite entity. By being nobody, the analyst can seem to be anybody; an enigma on which the patient can play variations. It may seem at first paradoxical that a patient's relation with others can best be improved by *not* knowing the person who is helping him rather than by knowing him. The comparative blankness of the analyst is, however, the quickest and most effective way of disinterring what is wrong with the patient's present relationships, in what way his human needs were not met in the past, and what he needs and hopes from human beings in the future.

Thus, psychoanalysis has a claim to be considered curative which rests both on its theoretical structure and also upon its therapeutic technique. Both these main features are incomplete. No one doubts that as we gradually come to know more of the actual nature of man as a biological phenomenon, the theoretical basis of psychoanalysis will alter. Nor can anyone fail to expect that techniques of transference interpretation will improve. Research will certainly disclose more of the nature of man's basic needs and instinctive development; and the more we know of this the more will interpretation be directed rightly to put patients in touch with that from which they are alienated.

There remains a final question, which is related to the problem of cure. We have admitted that psychoanalysis is a therapeutic technique which does not necessarily cure symptoms. Does it in fact make people worse?

There are two main fears which deter people from seeking analytical help who might otherwise do so. The first is that they will become intensely dependent on the analyst, unable to escape from his clutches, and thus ensnared in a necessarily unsatisfactory relation from which they cannot disentangle themselves. The second is that the analytical process will, by tracing the origin of their difficulties to their primary roots, destroy such adaptation as they have achieved, especially if this happens to be in the field of creative activity. The first fear is of course assuming that analysis is ineffective; the second that it is all too powerful an agent.

There is some weight in both these objections. It is certainly true that some patients become intensely dependent, and cannot easily be weaned from their attachment to the analyst. Every patient becomes in some sense dependent; for one cannot reveal oneself to another person three or four times a week over a long period without coming to depend on that person, however shadowy a figure he may be. However, it is fair to say that very dependent people will be dependent on someone or something in any case; and that the analytical process is specifically aimed at making people more self-reliant, not less. As we have said, the refusal of the analyst to act as a parent-substitute is one of the characteristics which best distinguishes analysis from other methods of help. Kindly persons who extend sympathy and compassion and who involve themselves deeply with another's predicament frequently find that they are in difficulties just because they attract a large number of dependent people whom they cannot wean and whose needs they cannot actually fulfil. The analyst may sometimes find himself in the same difficulty; but he, at least, is not attempting to fulfil the patient's needs direct, but only to help him to find his own solutions. The fact that some people are unable to do this is not to be laid at the door of analysis *per se*. However, we must admit that persistent, extreme dependency is a problem; and we have to accept that the needs of such people must be met in some other way, preferably by some kind of group or community organization. It is a fair criticism of analysis that it expects people to be more responsible and able to look after themselves than can be managed by quite a number of persons in any community.

The second objection is more cogent. If psychoanalysis is right in supposing that creative activity has its roots in primitive instinct, and if it is accepted that analytical technique is designed to enable patients to regain contact with their instinctive roots, and consequently to fulfil their basic needs direct, then it is proper to assume that some persons, at least, will abandon creative activity when they find that they can obtain instinctive satisfaction in other and less devious ways.

Creative activity, whether in the arts or in the sciences, is so characteristic of man and so uniquely human, that it is arguable that, however instinctive its origin, symbolic expression is a basic human need. Complexity, both of human society and of the brain itself, requires that men should express their natures in more subtle ways than those which they share with their animal cousins. The reduction of art to its instinctive roots does not destroy art, nor does it make it unnecessary. Psychoanalytic aesthetics have often been attacked on the grounds that, for example, the connection of Leonardo's paintings of the Virgin and St Anne with the fact that he had two mothers does nothing to explain his achievement. Indeed it does not; but this does not invalidate the interpretation. We all have to express our own natures in life as we live it, and if art is part of a valid way of expressing ourselves it will not be destroyed. What may be modified is the artistic activity of the person whose talent is insufficient to express himself effectively. We live in an age when to be creative is given so universal a prestige value that many are led to paint pictures or to write novels or to practise other arts who are insufficiently gifted to make this an effective way of expressing themselves. If analysis renders such people able to come to terms with their lack of talent and hence to abandon their creative efforts, it can do nothing but good. The talented need have no fears that analysis will take away from them something in which they have found a powerful and valid way of interacting with their environment.

To conclude, it seems reasonable to assert that psychoanalysis is best regarded as a method of semantic interpretation rather than a direct treatment for neurotic symptoms. The analytic process has value on two counts. First, the method of interpretation tends to present the patient with a scheme which, however incomplete, both makes sense of his distress and also tends to alleviate it by enabling him to come to terms with, and to express, his own instinctive nature. Second, psychoanalysis has a special claim to be superior to other methods of personal help in that the analyst is trained to interpret and resolve the transference. The question of cure is ultimately a philosophical one, since we know too little of the nature of man to be dogmatic about what constitutes the minimum requirements for psychological health; and the term 'cure' is in any case meaningless when we come to consider the manifold problems of the human condition, and the difficulties we all have in living. Psychoanalysis cannot solve all the problems implicit in the fact of being human. It can, however, and often does, both relieve distress and enable people to live and to work more effectively.

Love's Coming of Age

JOHN WREN-LEWIS

REVOLUTIONARIES notoriously become new oppressors in their turn, but it is supremely ironic that psychoanalysis, which began as the great instrument for liberating mankind from self-punishment and irrational guilt, should now be used by many people to make new rods for their own backs. Yet it undoubtedly happens. Personnel managers say that when single people over about twenty-five apply for jobs today they are often embarrassingly anxious to talk about their sex-lives, lest it be assumed that they are inadequate persons who have none: this is undoubtedly a side-effect of the psychoanalytic revelation of how crucial a role Eros plays in human psychology. The correspondence columns of family magazines reveal countless cases of mothers castigating themselves because they are merely human and have failed to bestow perfect loving care on their children: no previous generation of mothers has suffered in this way, because they did not have psychoanalysis to show them how neuroses, failures in learning and delinquency can be traced back to emotional deprivation or trauma in childhood.

No doubt it is journalism about psychoanalysis which is directly to blame for this kind of thing, rather than psychoanalysis itself, but the psychoanalytic movement cannot be held wholly innocent of responsibility for this inversion of its professed intentions. Most of its representatives would want to disassociate themselves firmly from the theories and methods of the priests who dealt with questions of guilt in earlier generations, but the fact is that the movement as a whole has inherited a streak of moral sadism from traditional religion, the presence of which sometimes becomes apparent in the very arguments that are used to criticize religion. The most notable example of this goes back to Freud himself, although it has been repeated by psychoanalytic spokesmen again and again—namely, the argument that psychoanalysis represents the third and final stage in the scientific revolution which has been stripping away mankind's religious delusions of grandeur over the past three centuries or so.[32] The first stage, so the argument runs, was the recognition by Copernicus and Galileo that the earth is not the centre of the stellar universe, but only a minor planet of a run-of-the-mill star in an inconceivably vast galaxy (which now turns out to be only one amongst myriads of others); then Darwin pushed the process a stage further by forcing us to recognize that man has no specially privileged place even on this planet, since he is only one more product of organic evolution depending on natural selection from chance variations; and today, the argument concludes, psychoanalysis is ramming the lesson right home, by showing how man's much-vaunted reason is always subservient to his emotional needs, and by finally exposing the pretensions of religion as a neurotic projection. Now this is actually a complete misrepresentation of what the scientific revolution in human thought has really been doing to man's sense of his own significance, and I think the mistake is a genuine case of the 'Freudian slip', in that it betrays a wish to be morally censorious about humanity, a desire to make people feel small, exactly parallel to the traditional theological castigation of man for sinful pride.

For, in truth, medieval theology did *not* give man delusions of grandeur about his place in the universe by its placing the earth at the centre of things. On the contrary, this centre was thought of as a very lowly place, to which mankind was supposed to be consigned because of a fall from grace : the only lower place in the medieval view was hell, which was held to be at the centre of the earth itself. The really important regions of the universe were the spheres beyond the sphere of the moon—the spheres of the planets, the sphere of the fixed stars, the *primum mobile* and, most remote of all, the heavenly realm where the Deity was supposed to dwell, the supremely important Being at the greatest distance of all from the centre. The destruction of medieval cosmology by Copernicus and Galileo was therefore in no sense a demotion of man from an exalted position in his own estimation of himself. For the vast majority of people it came as a great liberation, that they no longer felt bound to inevitable servitude in a social structure whose 'degrees' had hitherto been assumed to be part of a grand design running right through the universe—and at the same time, the new astronomy gave to mankind a tremendous sense of positive significance, in that it revealed a capacity in human beings to study and understand time and space on a scale never dreamt of in earlier philosophy.

Similarly, it is quite untrue to say that medieval theology gave man an exalted view of his place in the scale of living creatures. It actually set him very near the bottom of the scale, for it envisaged great ranges of living beings above man—angels, archangels, thrones, dominions, principalities, powers, cherubim and sera-phim—far outnumbering the orders of animal creation inferior to him. The ancient Eastern cosmologies did the same : some of them were using the idea of evolu-tion many centuries before Darwin, but they used it in the context of a doctrine of reincarnation and transmi-gration of souls, and they placed mankind at a very low stage in the process, with far more levels of astral and spiritual evolution above than there were of animal-spirits and plant-spirits below. The Darwinian revolution came as a blow to traditional religion not because it degraded man's place in the scale of life—the great religions had already done that—but because it destroyed the notion of the Great System in nature, by exposing the apparent 'order of creation' as merely a by-product of chance. Humanity acquired a new sense of dignity as the bringer of order into an otherwise random nature, and at the same time people were freed from the oppressive sense of having constantly to justify their ordinary lives by serving a vast cosmic purpose which dwarfed merely human values.

It is, of course, possible that Freud (and others who have argued in the same vein about the Copernican and Darwinian revolutions, such as, for example, Bertolt Brecht) simply did not know the facts about ancient cosmology. Psychoanalysis itself, however, would lead us to suspect that such a straightforward explanation is unlikely to be the whole story when major misinterpretations like these are involved, amounting almost to inversion of the truth. And in fact Freud's extension of the 'stripping-away-mankind's-delusions-of-grandeur' argument to his own revolutionary discoveries involved just as great a misinterpretation in respect of the human significance of traditional religious ideas about psychology, although he could scarcely have been ignorant in this field. The traditional religious idea of reason as the supreme mental faculty was in no way a high view of human dignity. The essence of reason in this sense is its impersonality, and the classical exaltation of intellect implied the insignificance of all merely personal considerations before the laws of the Great System of the World. Man's highest good, on this view, was to arrive by logic at the pre-ordained truth about the Great System so as to adapt himself to it. The scientific revolution which began in Galileo's time was a demotion of this kind of reason right from the beginning, for its key feature was subordination of logic to the experimental method, and experiment is fundamentally an assertion of man's capacity to alter the natural pattern of things in accordance with his own human inclinations and imaginings. The fact that the experimental method has succeeded, even to the point of enabling psychoanalysis to emerge and expose the way in which logic on its own tends to rationalize acceptance of the *status quo* by providing symbolic pseudo-satisfactions for people's emotional needs—this fact gives man a significance infinitely greater than the traditional religious assertions about his godlike reason. It means he has to take himself seriously as a creative animal, and the psychoanalytic exposure of religion as in essence a mechanism for avoiding responsibility points to precisely the same conclusion.

The discovery that men's ideas of gods, demons, angels and other metaphysical principles are projections of inner fantasies undoubtedly dispels a delusion, but to call it a delusion of grandeur is to take over, consciously or unconsciously, religion's own valuation of inner feelings and fantasies as worthless in their own right, meaningful only in so far as they are believed to reflect a spiritual universe outside the individual human psyche. Part of Freud unconsciously took over this value judgement and bequeathed a censorious, quasi-religious legacy to the psychoanalytic movement which it has even now not wholly outgrown, although the main impetus of Freud's discoveries is in the *opposite* direction—towards overthrowing the paranoia of the religious outlook completely, and recognizing the feelings and fantasies of the inner life as autonomous facts of the universe worthy of being taken seriously in themselves. (By paranoia I mean living your life under the persecutory delusion that events are somehow being controlled from behind the scenes.) For what actually emerges in analysis is that the religious philosophy which explains moods and feelings by reference to astrological or other metaphysical powers is a device for evading the fact that the moods and feelings are part of what we are; the desire for another world in which the soul can be free of the sordid entanglements of physical nature is a way of avoiding the difficulties of coping with the physical world and trying to make it less unpleasant; the effort to adjust all life to the supposed decrees of a father-god is a device for escaping from the inner fact of being at once dependent and dictatorial; and the worship of an ever-loving saviour is a means of dodging the difficulties of particular human relationships with their continual ambivalence. Beliefs about metaphysical realities are delusions of smallness, not of grandeur, from the point of view of their implications for human psychology : religion is the universal neurosis of humanity because it enables people to avoid facing the awful fact that they and all their feelings and fantasies are significant. In fact it is necessary to recognize that the decline of religious belief over the past three centuries was actually a precondition rather than a product of the new advances in science, for although particular discoveries like those of Copernicus and Darwin undoubtedly helped to spread doubts about specific doctrines in Christian theology, at bottom there must have been a move away from preoccupation with metaphysical ideas, with a corresponding acceptance of human inclinations and imaginings as significant, for anyone to be prepared to use the experimental method in the first place. The scientific revolution, with its demotion of traditional reason in favour of experiment, was from the outset a sign that humanity's universal neurosis had for some reason begun to recede, and the exposure of the neurosis itself by psychoanalysis in our own day should properly be seen as completing the revolution *by bringing into public consciousness this underlying psychological motif of growing human self-confidence.*

I believe one of the most important tasks facing the psychoanalytic movement today is to revalue itself along these lines, not only for its own sake but for the sake of our whole culture, lest we suffer regression to the universal neurosis in a new form. For there is a new form of collective paranoia incipient in our society, and Freud's argument about stripping away mankind's delusions of grandeur points directly towards it. It is called scientific materialism, and it consists of giving metaphysical significance to the concepts used by modern science, so as to present a picture of the universe as a Great System of physical forces, and of human beings as mere by-products of those forces.

This philosophy represents itself as the ultimate opponent of religion, but psychologically speaking it is merely a new form of religion; this emerges very clearly in that most famous statement of the scientific material- ist's *credo*, Bertrand Russell's essay *A Free Man's Worship*,[73] which John Gilmour has suggested ought properly to be conceived as a poem :

> Brief and powerless is Man's life;
> On him and all his race
> The slow, sure doom falls
> Pitiless and dark.
> Blind to good and evil;
> Reckless of destruction,
> Omnipotent matter rolls on its relentless way;

Scientific materialism normally does not use this kind of language : it masquerades as a "cold, unemotional, objective conclusion" drawn directly from what science has actually discovered. In fact, science has not dis- covered anything of the kind, for it is of its very essence anti-metaphysical. Its concepts of matter, energy and force are not discoveries but intellectual models used, always on a strictly provisional basis, to suggest new and complicated lines of experimental action : of their very essence they imply man as a creative agent, and every success achieved by science in using them is a vin- dication of man as a creative agent. There could really be no greater nonsense than to suggest that man is noth- ing but a by-product of material forces, for the material forces of today's science are quite different from those of yesterday, and will almost certainly be different again tomorrow. The constant factor in modern science is not Omnipotent Matter but Potent Man: Omnipotent Matter is a metaphysical construct which provides, as Russell's passage shows quite clearly, an admirable excuse for avoiding the responsibility of taking human desires really seriously, exactly as Omnipotent God did in earlier generations.

The fact that Russell himself has not taken much advantage of this excuse in his work and life, any more than Freud or many others who expressed similar ideas, merely shows that great men have the greatness to be inconsistent. The philosophy of scientific materialism can and does cause genuine harm, both by providing a direct excuse for cynical utilitarianism and political manipulation (which we now know from psychoanalysis to be just as much ways of escape from taking the real feelings of the inner life seriously as neurotic religiosity is) and also by confusing people of a humanist or artistic turn of mind into thinking that science is their enemy. There can be no greater paradox than the tendency of many artists and educationalists at the present time to see modern science and technology as threats to the development of sensitive, feeling, creative human beings. The very essence of experiment is an act of creation, bringing something new into existence that never was on land or sea: and technology should be the means by which people are set free from utilitarian drudgery to sense and feel as never before, with their artistic powers extended to a scale never dreamt of in traditional philosophy. Moreover, both science and technology require the gifts of sensitivity and humane awareness even to succeed in their own fields: the greatest advances in science take place through cross-fertilization from widely separate fields of discourse, sometimes from outside science altogether,[59] while every technological project requires co-operation of specialist skills and personal gifts at every level for its successful completion (to say nothing of the fact that it is utterly profitless unless it springs from at least some awareness of human need). The irony is complete when people try to combat materialism by reviving religion and harking back to the values of pre-scientific cultures to counteract the influence of science in education. The truth is that materialism is a form of religion, and the inhumanities of materialistic society, whether totalitarian or commercial, are often precisely the same as the inhumanities of traditional religious societies—compulsion, pressure of guilt, regimentation. The way to combat materialism is not to try to go back on the scientific revolution in any way, but to take that revolution really seriously, at both the intellectual and the social levels. Intellectually this means recognizing that scientific ideas are always *suggestions for action* in a universe which is seen experimentally as a Great Opportunity rather than as any kind of Great System. On the social plane, it means recognizing that technological power by its very nature implies that, at this practical level also, systems are made for man, not man for systems.

It is worth adding that many of the latest developments both in science and in technology cry out for man to take himself seriously as a creative animal in this way. In fundamental science, for example, it seems as if progress is made precisely at the point where physicists do consciously give up the effort to interpret theories as descriptions of some ultimate universal system underlying the ordinary world of experience, and accept the

94

possibility of using mutually contradictory concepts like 'wave' and 'particle' for different purposes: it also seems as if the only kind of statement that can be made about the basic structure of the world is that it is indeed a world of potentiality, a world of almost limitless possibilities where the only ultimate laws to be observed are the statistical laws of chance. On the plane of more practical science there are a whole range of modern developments which suggest that scientists have only to define something as impossible, against the laws of the system, for other scientists to make it happen in an unexpected way: one of the basic certainties of chemistry used to be that the so-called inert gases (neon, xenon, etc.) *were* inert, but today they form compounds, while in the biological realm it seems that germ-plasm has almost limitless possibilities of novelty in it, enabling seeds, for example, to grow in atmospheres that were thought to be unable to support life because the ordinary living plants died in them. And parallel with all this, in the realm of technological practice, industrial development is rapidly reaching the stage where it becomes possible, even organizationally advantageous, for systems to be based on recognition of people's inner life of feeling and fantasy instead of requiring its suppression. The old machines, both physical and social, were merely modernized versions of traditional, ritualistic patterns of organizing work and social life, and so tended to resist any efforts people might make to assert themselves as feeling, creative persons: the promise today is of machines so subtle that they will positively require people to do so.

On the other hand, it is perfectly possible to force all these developments into a metaphysical/impersonal framework, materialistic or religious, if the will to do so is

strong enough, or the will to do otherwise is insufficiently strong. It is ultimately only at the psychological
level that the neurotic retreat into metaphysics can really
be prevented, and it is therefore of the utmost interest
and importance to see just how it has come about that
some of the basic assumptions of humanity's universal
neurosis have got themselves carried over into the very
movement in which modern scientific methods have un-
masked the universal neurosis, the psychoanalytic movement. The reason, as I have tried to show, is a moral/
emotional matter rather than a purely intellectual one.
Philosophical critics of Freud sometimes say that he
inherited a materialistic bias from nineteenth-century
physics, but statements like this merely evade the really
interesting question, which is why anyone, even the
nineteenth-century physicists, should ever have interpreted concepts of experimental science in metaphysical
terms so as to construct a materialist system. For the
nineteenth-century physicists it might be plausible merely
to say that the modern scientific movement had not in
their day been going for long enough to dispel the
ingrained habits of metaphysical interpretation in the
public philosophy, but such a simple answer can hardly
apply to Freud, who had actually exposed the neurotic
character of the metaphysical way of thinking. *It follows
that if we can see what happened when Freud allowed
some basic assumptions of humanity's universal neurosis
to carry over into his thought, we shall be seeing something of the root cause of the universal neurosis itself.*
And from this it might be reasonable to hope for insight
into why that neurosis began to recede at the time of the
Renaissance, and what might be done in our own day to
move towards completion of the cure. In finding the
solution to its own internal problem, psychoanalysis

could make its crowning contribution to the future of mankind, for the curing of the universal neurosis is the essential precondition for the cure of any of mankind's other ills.

Up to now the question of just why humanity fell into the neurosis of religion right from the beginning of its history has mostly been passed over. In so far as psychoanalytic thinkers have considered it at all, they have almost always been content with Freud's own answer, that it was a simple defence-mechanism against the unpleasant fact of man's insignificance and powerlessness in the universe. But this, of course, presupposes the metaphysical view itself, the very view which is confounded by the fact that science and psychoanalysis exist at all. The fact that man has it in him to find the universe unpleasant, alien and terrifying means that he also has it in him to change things, and all the evidence of the past three centuries goes to show that wherever he is prepared to accept the challenge, he can sooner or later rise to it and find the power to change things. And indeed if that kind of diagnosis were to be given of an ordinary individual neurosis, any psychoanalyst worth his salt would question it as likely to be altogether too superficial : to say that a patient indulges in paranoid fantasies because he finds the reality-situation too much for him would in most cases be to miss altogether the really important question of *why* he finds it too much for him. A deeper and much more positive reason would be sought, and I believe that in the case of humanity's universal neurosis we can find just such a reason, emerging into public view in the paradox I have been discussing in Freud's thought, from which the psychoanalytic movement has not yet freed itself. I have already indicated, right at the outset of this essay, what

I believe the underlying cause of this paradox to be—namely, moral sadism, the wish to make people feel small (of which moral masochism, the wish to wallow in a sense of self-reproach at one's own insignificance, is merely the obverse side). My suggestion is that this is no mere local foible of the psychoanalytic movement, but the underlying reason for mankind's age-long tendency to pervert the distinctive human gift of imagination from its proper functioning in creative activity, to the paranoid fantasying of occult worlds and powers.

There has, of course, been no lack of awareness in the psychoanalytic movement of the neurotic character of moral sadism : indeed, the very essence of psychoanalytic practice is that neuroses can be brought into the open and coped with only by virtue of a deliberate suspension, in the analyst–patient relationship, of society's normal moralizing tendencies. Moreover, I have heard more than one analyst say that although it is possible to cope (given enough time, skill and luck) with even the nastiest of 'immoral' feelings, and in principle to deal with even the deepest childhood fears, the one thing that is absolutely certain to prevent progress towards health is an insistence by the patient on clinging to moralistic attitudes towards himself or others. But I believe the full significance of these basic facts of psychoanalytic practice has mostly been missed. Moral sadism has usually been interpreted as a secondary phenomenon, a by-product of the complex power-relations between the young child and its parents (or its fantasies of its parents). Valuable as it may be to analyse these relations in individual cases, however, to take them as fundamental determinants of neurosis is to pass over the most interesting and crucial fact that the fantasy-life of infants does function in this way rather than some other way. In man, evolution seems to have produced a creature with a new way of approaching its environment (its direct perceptions passing over at all points into prolific free-wheeling fantasies) which in the earliest days and months has terrible difficulties in functioning properly (turning to anger and fear, for example, when parents go away, unable merely to rest content until they return) : if, as seems likely, all neurosis goes back to this crucial malfunctioning, then the really fundamental need is to detect and define the precise way in which the malfunctioning begins at its roots. And this is just the issue with which we are confronted in considering moral sadism, for although it is certainly important in individual cases to trace back specific neurotic moralizing symptoms to infantile punitive fantasies occasioned by anxiety and deprivation, to leave the matter there in fundamental psychological theory is to pass over the extraordinary fact that the infant should ever have punitive fantasies, or, for that matter, that parents should ever punish.

Punishment and revenge are not natural things. On the adult level, we already know that punishment is not what it usually claims to be, a straightforward learning discipline : as a learning discipline it is usually worse than ineffective, producing the very opposite of the effects that are intended, because of the strong counter-reactions it brings about.[7] The animal kingdom manages its learning without anything that can really be called punishment, because adults of the animal kingdom apparently do not carry over from *their* childhood vengeful punitive fantasies that confuse the whole business of training. The significant thing about this neurosis is altogether missed, however, if the extra component is merely attributed to aggression, whether in the unconscious fantasies of the adult or in the vengeful fantasies of the infant from which they spring. Aggression in the animal world is a limited thing, with highly specific occasions and relatively straightforward discharge.[8] The point at which aggression in man becomes the dangerous, frenzied, inordinate thing it is, is precisely the point at which it becomes punishment or revenge and begins to acquire the peculiar flavour contained in words like 'judgement', 'ought', 'deserving' and 'guilt' which, as the moral philosophers have long since shown, cannot in any way be logically equated with 'anger', 'must', 'vulnerable' or 'fear'. I believe that in order to get our thinking about human life straight, it is necessary to recognize that moral scorn is something fundamental in man's distinctively human nature : it is the negative counterpart of the autonomy and creativity which make man what he is, and it defines the point at which animal aggression becomes human destructiveness, just as creativity and autonomy define the point at which animal sex-urges and parental-urges become human love. In this sense moralism has, as the moral philosophers point out, a kind of absoluteness about it, a sense of being an end in itself rather than a means to discipline or anything like that : in this it directly resembles love, but what moral philosophers usually fail to see is that moral scorn is actually a negative, not a positive absolute, as love is. The modern thinker who came nearest to seeing this clearly was probably George Orwell, in the famous passage at the close of *1984*[71] where he enunciated the basic principle of inhumanity, that "The end of cruelty is cruelty, the end of torture is torture." To be accurate, I believe this should be transposed to "The end of punishment is punishment, the end of scorn is scorn," but the effect, as Orwell's O'Brien states quite explicitly, is to destroy the distinctively human thing about man and reduce him to a cell in the body of the herd.

Freud himself did in fact have an inkling, towards the end of his life, of this crucial negative role of moral sadism and masochism. In his earlier work he was for the most part content to treat the moral urge as an introjection of parental discipline, and he dealt with the curious character of guilt by the expedient (logically quite fallacious) of pushing its ultimate origin back in time to the tribal dawn of the human race.[24] His famous myth about the sons of the tribe killing their father and thereafter bequeathing to the human race an inherited sense of sin begged the question, as has often been pointed out, of why on earth the sons should ever have felt guilty in the first place if their only fear was of their father's strength—and, of course, this question can be appropriately re-stated if the myth is interpreted in terms of individual fantasy-history, as tends to happen in more modern psychoanalytic theory. In his later work, however, Freud began to see that there must be something much more fundamental involved, and he expressed this, in the almost equally mythological language of his more developed theories, by saying he had come to the conclusion that the formation of the super-ego, the moral conscience, involved some absolutely basic negative principle which he called the death-wish, a principle far more negative than mere aggression.[30] He went on to try to fit this idea into a materialist meta-physic, by interpreting it as something like the inbuilt urge of all living materials to return to the inorganic state; he also toyed with the notion that the interplay of the death-instinct (*Thanatos*) and the love-instinct (*Eros*) might be a manifestation at the human level of the negative and positive forces of electricity. These speculations have brought his whole idea of a death-wish into discredit in subsequent psychoanalytic thought, but in the midst of this metaphysical bath-water, which we can let go happily, there seems to me to be a baby of insight which is of the utmost importance. The metaphysical language points to it, yet at the same time obscures it. The truth is that moral sadism is not a *product* of some occult negative force, but a negative principle in itself, the fundamental turning of the spontaneity of the inner life against itself.

Now, of course, this idea has only to be stated to awaken an echo of a very much older statement, the ancient Hebrew myth that mankind suffers from a universal alienation that is rooted in 'knowledge of good and evil'. I would suggest that this is an instance, on the social plane, of the psychoanalytic principle that the major fantasy-themes thrown up by a neurosis contain important hints of its fundamental cause and cure, even though the neurotic sufferer himself cannot see their meaning. For this particular myth, the story of Adam and Eve, is central to the major manifestation of humanity's universal neurosis in the Western world, the Christian system (almost more central there, paradoxically, than in Judaism);[83] yet it has never, within that system, been understood according to its most obvious meaning. It has been made the occasion for imposing enormous guilt-feelings about sex on people, although the story says nothing whatever about sex being any reason for guilt;[3] it has been made the occasion for moral suppression of cultural and scientific initiative on the ground that this is a manifestation of 'sinful pride', although the story quite plainly suggests that man fulfils himself by exercising dominion over nature, and even goes so far as to say that it is man's destiny to determine what names things shall have instead of taking these as given by any sort of divine writ in nature (actually a fairly precise myth of technology). In general, the story of the loss of Eden has been made the occasion for imposing rigid moralistic suppression of many different kinds on people, although the core of the story is a statement that moralizing is the one absolutely certain way for human spontaneity and creativity to destroy itself ("Of the tree of knowledge of good and evil ye shall not eat, or ye shall surely die"). In the characteristic manner of neurotic rationalization, the moralistic suppression has been justified as a necessary means to human welfare ('keeping a rein on men's destructive impulses so as to make life tolerable') but in practice has served to rationalize inhumanity (for example, by giving a kind of ritual justification to aggressive impulses in war or tyranny) instead of curing or even restricting it.

Of course, there have from time to time been individuals who have in some measure seen through the pretensions of moralistic culture, and it is interesting that in Jewish/Christian cultural traditions a notable number of these prophetic figures have appealed to the plain meaning of the Adam and Eve story as the basis for a revolt against their current religious Establishment. The most notable example of this was the founder of Christianity himself, whose whole career was a revolt against the religious system of his society, based on what he believed to be the 'true meaning' of the Judaic ideas underlying that system : a great many of his attacks on, and offences to, the system were protests against moralism—"Judge not, lest ye be judged"; "Condemn not those that condemn you"; "Why callest thou me good?"; "Let him who is without sin cast the first stone"; "I agreed with every man a penny". It was not long before people had found ways of accommodating this to a new system of moralistic metaphysics, but the fact that the root of mankind's universal neurosis had come so near to public exposure at this point may well have had something to do, I think, with the fact that Jesus of Nazareth became the starting-point for an entirely new religion of his own with enormous universal appeal, instead of merely being absorbed into the relatively unimportant Hebrew tradition as earlier prophetic rebels had been. Moreover, it seems to me even more significant that it was to be from Christendom that, after sixteen centuries or so, the strange new movement called the scientific revolution was to come to birth, with its astonishing evidence of a major (and continuing) recession in the universal neurosis. I believe there is a direct connection between this and the fact that Christendom, in some ways the most comprehensive system of moralistic metaphysics the world has ever known, has also carried a contradiction at its heart as no other system has done. Right at the outset Paul of Tarsus, a moralizing metaphysician if ever there was one, was driven to produce analysis after analysis in his letters showing the futility of moralizing, and it is worth noting that he was also led to make one of the greatest poetic assertions of man's destiny as a creative animal to be found anywhere in our literature—the myth in the Letter to the Romans of nature as a creature in bondage, groaning and travailing, waiting to be set free by man realizing in himself the kind of creative power that religion ordinarily attributes to God. In later centuries prophetic rebels began to appear more and more frequently, appealing to this and kindred statements in the New Testament writings to protest in one way or another against the orthodox theological vision of the Great System, and at the period when the scientific revolution was beginning to dawn they were coming thick and fast. Peter Abelard, for instance, set the tone of the Renaissance when he appealed to the statement flung off in the New Testament that men ought themselves to be creative beings, like gods; and in the period of the scientific revolution itself one of the great English pioneers, Francis Bacon, appealed to the Adam and Eve story to state a theme which would undermine the whole structure of everything Christendom had hitherto stood for :

> For man by the Fall fell at the same time from his state of innocency and from his dominion over nature. Both of these losses, however, can even in this life be in some part repaired; the former by religion and faith, the latter by the arts and sciences.

Moreover, it was usually the case that the prophets who appealed to the New Testament in order to rebel against Christendom's theological system also found themselves appealing to other recorded sayings of Jesus to attack Christian moralism. Perhaps the most outstanding case in England, in the first heyday of the scientific revolution, was that strange figure William Blake, who incidentally was prophetic enough to see the danger that scientific teaching might have the effect of exchanging the neurosis of Christian theology for an equal neurosis of mechanistic materialism. His most constant theme was the attack on moralism in the name of the teachings of Jesus :

> If Moral Virtue was Christianity,
> Christ's Pretensions were all Vanity.

It seems to me most apt that one of the stories associated with the founder of Christianity in the New

Testament is a suggestion that his ideas would be buried by people who turned him into a religious figure (saying "Lord, Lord"), but that those ideas would nevertheless work away in the world like leaven until society as a whole suddenly awoke to find itself in process of a total revolution against mankind's universal alienation. Christianity seems to me to have been indeed the religion destined to end religion, to quote Marx's famous expression—and this idea is anticipated (again without most Christians having been able to see it) in the myth that stands at the other end of our Bible, the myth of the Book of Revelation, which envisages a new age when mankind would have no more use for temples. Marx's own vision of the end of humanity's universal neurosis stopped short at a recognition of man's creativity on the purely social level, with the result that he did not himself succeed in laying bare the real roots either of religion or of social tyranny; indeed, his followers have gone further than any other movement in the Western world in developing the religious potentialities of scientific materialism into something like an actual organized religion. It was with Freud, that other Hebrew prophet of the scientific revolution, that real insight into the universal neurosis began finally to break surface. He recognized that the root of human alienation lies not in economics or politics but in personal life itself, at the most intimate level where each person faces (or avoids facing) his own inner life, and is involved in relationships with other individuals on the basis of recognizing them (or directly refusing to recognize them) as beings with the same kind of inner life. It is at this level that political tyranny begins, in compensation for failures of personal life, and it is even at this level that economic enslavement begins, when creativity fails and man be-

comes enslaved to mere minimal cultivation of nature
instead of rising to the kind of creative exploitation of
it which can give wealth for all instead of a handful.
Marx saw religion's misdirection of human aspirations
only from the outside, and was content for the most
part to think of it as a secondary phenomenon, a propa-
ganda device of rulers, whereas Freud saw into the
inner nature of the matter and recognized it as a neurotic
condition gripping rulers and ruled alike. He gained
much of his insight by penetrating to the truth revealed
yet concealed in mankind's collective fantasies, most
notably the myths of ancient Greece. It is ironic (though
with psychoanalytic hindsight not perhaps surprising)
that he never really saw through to the fundamental
insight hidden in the myths of his own race (including
that special section of the race which latter-day Jews
so often find it hard to acknowledge, the New Testament Christian Jews). I believe psychoanalysis is now
in a position to use that insight, and in doing so to
bring to completion the process of healing that has been
working itself out in Christendom since Jesus of Nazareth
sowed the first seeds of enlightenment about the need for
love to abolish moralization.

For the story of humanity for most of its history *is* the
story of Adam and Eve. It is the story of people cower-
ing under visions of wrathful divinity, alienated from
sex and oppressed by nature. It is the story of people
mentally dissociated from bodily life so that instinct
seems like a threat (the flaming sword that turned every
way—as nice a symbol of dissociated erotic aggression
as one could wish for). It is the story of people bringing
up children whose anxieties can lead to murder. And all
these things have happened because the inevitable con-
comitant of the human stage in evolution is the possibility

that spontaneity can deny itself, by seeking as it were to control itself and the response of others, and this is the act of moral judgement which must, of its very nature, stultify creativity (making man feel a slave of nature instead of its potential master) and, on the other side of the coin, introduce defence-mechanisms (fig-leaves) which frustrate love. It is a significant feature of theological interpretations of the Adam and Eve story that they almost always ignore the presence of Eve, except as a source of temptation : in religious language, human alienation is normally referred to as the Sin of Adam. From the psychological point of view the equal presence of Adam and Eve in the story is one of its most interesting features. The point in human life where things go right or wrong is the point at which the indi-vidual *encounters another individual* on the basis of a communication in terms of personal autonomy : neither fulfilment nor deprivation can be understood on the level of individuality in isolation, any more than they can be understood on the level of purely external social or economic relationship in society. One of the most paradoxical effects of the materialist-metaphysical bias on psychoanalysis has been the fact that its theory has so largely tended to treat love purely as a kind of blind biological drive or appetite, although psychoanalytic practice has done more than moralists have ever done to make people aware (at any rate specific people actu-ally under analysis) that a relationship which involves no real human contact, at the level where communication about the spontaneity of the inner life takes place, is not a satisfying expression of *Eros* at all. This is the basic reason why it is almost worse than useless to try to pre-vent 'love-deprivation' in childhood by making mothers feel worried and guilty about any kind of 'selfishness' that might lead to acts of neglect : even the tiny infant needs not just material care and fondling (as might be appropriate with rhesus monkeys), nor lots of emotion left to communicate itself by some telepathic magic, but love in the sense of personal concern communicated through countless tiny acts of creative initiative. *Eros* is the urge towards personal mutuality, and it is crucial to psychological health because it is simply the other side of the coin of individual integrity and creativeness. Psychological health can be defined equally well as taking oneself seriously as a creative autonomous being or as having a satisfactory love-life, for the two definitions imply each other. Love at the human level means creative communication in some form or other, and an act of creation means an act of mutuality. Even at the crudest technological level, as I have said, an invention is of no use unless it meets some kind of human need, and this is always at the end of the day a matter of improving human relationships. A man who stirs a pond is producing novelty, but we do not call him an inventor; a genuine invention implies mutuality even if only at the fairly abstract level of giving a wide range of people new material objects to enrich (or otherwise) the ordinary communication of their daily lives. The nature of the creative act itself is most clearly seen, however, when it takes place in the context of some direct personal relationship, as when the cooking of a meal or the writing of a poem opens up new areas in the communication of an Adam and an Eve. When I used the term Potent Man earlier, the Freudian *double entendre* was unconscious, but certainly significant.

The other feature of the story which becomes of great interest from the psychological point of view because it is totally misrepresented in theological interpretations,

is the character of God. What is palpably obvious, but
never admitted in any theological approach, is that the
character of God *changes* with the eating of the dangerous fruit, and this makes perfect sense if the story is
interpreted as a myth about human experience *seen
essentially from the human viewpoint,* like a dream.
After Adam and Eve have eaten the fruit, God appears
as the God of theology—a punitive, repressive controller
of natural events, who (absurdly) is worried about Adam
and Eve's capacity to seize that control (the Tree of
Life), in spite of the fact that on any theological view
he must have been responsible for giving them this
capacity! *Before* they come to know good and evil, on
the other hand, God is represented altogether differently:
walking with Adam and Eve in the garden, and asserting that man should have dominion over the earth and
find names for things; he warns about the fatal character of the Tree of Knowledge of Good and Evil, but
says nothing about not touching the Tree of Life, which
is by implication included amongst the range of choices
which man should freely exercise to fulfil himself. The
meaning seems plain: God before the Fall is a symbol
of the fundamental energy of personal life, the energy
of *Eros,* and the story is a perfect myth of the way in
which man becomes alienated from *Eros* by the knowledge of good and evil, following which the image of
Eros is projected into the Beyond and endowed with the
qualities of the very principle that leads to the alienation, the principle of moralizing. Freud's own myth of
Eros taking on in alienation the characteristics of his
'eternal antagonist', *Thanatos,* expresses precisely this
truth, but if anything less clearly. William Blake expressed it too, when he spoke of mankind worshipping
Satan as God, and wrote of the true God:

Love's Coming of Age

Thou art a Man, God is no more,
Thine own Humanity learn to Adore.

The idea that the image of God in myths and individual fantasies might occasionally stand for something other than a paranoid projection of fatherhood, power and authority was, of course, one of the suggestions for modifying psychoanalytic theory made by the best-known of Freud's followers, C. G. Jung, but it seems to me that he expressed it in terms which justified Freud in rejecting it. The debate that took place between Freud and Jung on this score was indeed just one aspect of a general issue between them which is directly relevant to the theme I have been exploring in this essay—the theme of taking man's inner life seriously in its own right, and the insidious temptation for even psychologists to avoid this by lapsing into metaphysics. For underlying all Jung's detailed suggestions for modifying psychoanalytic theory was a basic concern to insist that the inner life *should* be taken seriously in its own right and not be devalued, either in psychotherapy or in the general public philosophy, by the metaphysical bias of materialism; but in his efforts to achieve this objective Jung evolved a mythology of his own which, as Freud instantly saw, pointed straight back to older, religious forms of metaphysics. In particular, Jung called for a clear recognition that the fantasies of the inner life could have significance in terms of an individual's creative enterprise as well as in terms of his fixation in infantile conflicts; fantasies of a commanding yet alluring and evasive female might be signs of a mother-fixation, but they might also, Jung maintained, be at the same time signs of a beckoning inspiration, and *either* of these things could complicate a man's ordinary sex-life. Following this line of thought, Jung began an interesting study of what might be called the natural history of human creative processes, teasing out, from comparisons of patients' dreams and fantasies with literature, legends and myths, some of the great 'archetypal' patterns into which people's attitudes to the world tend to fall in different circumstances.[52] [54] The idea proved an exciting and fruitful one for people concerned with the arts, but its value was diminished even at this level, and almost totally vitiated in the actual field of psychoanalytic theory by the way Jung chose to express it; he said that fantasies considered in this light were expressions of 'the objective psyche', a term which is logically and psychologically indistinguishable from the religious notion of a spiritual world behind the scenes, since it conveys a psychic 'something' known only by its symbolic self-revelations.[20]

In fact Jung concentrated his criticisms on materialism as such rather than on the thing that is really wrong with materialism, its paranoid metaphysical character, and so he failed to see that the inner life is devalued just as much if referred to objective forces that are called 'psychic' as if it is explained in terms of biological instincts. He was led into the practical position of believing that because the old religious cultures paid more attention to myth and symbol, they were therefore in themselves taking mankind's inner creative life more seriously than modern scientific culture (or orthodox psychoanalysis) does,[51] and he even went so far as to urge, in a famous lecture delivered in England, that twentieth-century man's great need was to recover religion in the strictly practical sense of 'the symbolic life', a way of living in which every action, relationship, thought or feeling is given meaning by its symbolic role in some great cosmic drama—the absolute opposite of his initial intention of giving serious attention to human creativity in its own right.[53] Freud was not slow to see the paranoid character of these ideas and so reacted against Jung with great violence. The truth that both were concerned about got lost between them in their debate, as each pointed to the metaphysical beam in the other's eye while quite failing to see that he had one in his own. It should be added, however, that in more recent years the *rapprochement* that has taken place between the main psychoanalytic movement and the splinter-movement that formed to follow Jung has produced some of the most creative advances in the subject as a whole, although so far most of the advance has been at the strictly practical level of psychotherapeutic practice, and we are only just beginning to see the emergence of tentative theoretical formulations that really do manage to do justice to man as a creative animal (ego analysis) and to take the inner life seriously in its own right (existential analysis). Perhaps in one way this book as a whole is a contribution to that process.

The question of a possible positive value in the idea of God was in a way central to the Jung/Freud debate, because the sense of absoluteness which attaches to the idea of God comes very close to the sense of being an end in itself, which Jung wanted psychoanalysis to take seriously in relation to man's inner life. Jung formulated this by calling the image of God "the archetype of the Self", the symbol of the fundamental personal integrity which could emerge with the overcoming of neurotic ego-defences. He also suggested that the God-image might on occasions symbolize the basic energy of personal life, *libido*, which he saw could not be identified with a purely biological sex-drive. In his desire to put these ideas forward in opposition to materialism, however, he came to pay less and less attention to Freud's vital insight into the paranoid use to which religion has actually put its myths and theologies. He came to think of the practical business of analysis as an extension, a fulfilment, or perhaps even a recovery, of what religious disciplines such as prayer and meditation had provided for real devotees and mystics in earlier cultures, and he began to introduce ideas based on religious practice into analysis itself. He could never see why his apparently reasonable suggestions for modifying psychoanalytic theory should have evoked from Freud an apoplectic protest that this was opening the flood-gates to "the black tide of mud" of occultism, and it seemed to him that the founder of psychoanalysis must have had an almost religious fixation on sex in insisting that the only safeguard against the black tide was to "hold on to the sexual theory at all costs".[55]

What *we* can see now, with the perspective of distance, is that Freud was quite properly protesting that insights to be derived from religious ideas must always be treated first and foremost as insights about neurosis, since religion *is* the universal neurosis of humanity, an avoidance of those very values of personal significance and creativeness for which Jung was so anxious to stand. Realization of those values requires complete abandonment of all projection of fantasies into supposed occult realities, and recognition that fulfilment of the inner life comes in the mutualities of *Eros*. These are basic truths, neglect of which does indeed mean going back on everything psychoanalysis has achieved. The question Freud never considered (and Jung never seems to have raised) is whether it might not be possible to see Jung's insights about the idea of God in terms of these basic psychoanalytic truths instead of in neo-religious terms. My suggestion is that this is possible, and that the myths of the Jewish-Christian religious tradition in particular require this additional insight for their full understanding, because they actually depict, underneath the contradictions of normal theological interpretations, both the genesis and the possible cure of religion as alienation from *Eros*.

All religions of course contain myths about alienation, and some of the great Eastern myths resemble the Adam and Eve story in linking both 'knowledge of good and evil' and the worship of gods with the fact of alienation, although none that I have come across spells out the details of the causal sequence so clearly as the Hebrew one does. When it comes to myths about the cure of neurosis, however, the myths of the Hebrew/Christian tradition are unique in setting the fact of inner life firmly in the perspective of social history : they speak, not merely of the individual soul overcoming alienation, but of the possibility of a new age in human history when there need be no desire for temples because mankind as a whole has been set free from its age-long bondage to delusion. Corresponding to this, they depict the desirable goal not as a vague general condition of blessedness in which the soul acquires new powers and 'rises above good and evil' by virtue of some kind of enlightenment, but as a dynamic social condition in which mankind takes on 'dominion over nature' and the creative role that has traditionally been thought of as God's, *by virtue of finding a new mode of living in which love is able to contain moral sadism instead of being destroyed by it*.[42] Mankind's hope, say the myths, is of a new age when God is 'with us' as he was 'with' Adam and Eve in the Garden before the fall; in this new age, mankind's dominion over nature need know no bounds, so that there might be hope of dealing even with the basic natural aggressiveness whereby the wolf devours the lamb; man might even find that he has it in him to control disease and ageing, the corruptibility of the physical body; and the clue to it all would be 'forgiveness', a mode of life in which the fundamental relations between people pass beyond moralizing to a new approach to love wherein even the terrible fruits of alienation are accepted, not judged. Now so long as these myths are treated theologically they are almost worse than useless, but it seems to me that the great significance of Jesus of Nazareth in our history was that he saw through the theological interpretations of contemporary Judaism and realized—or at least came very near to realizing—something of what they really meant. That was why he went around talking about having Good News for mankind, and urging that the New Age could come at any time (or at least, he behaved in ways that led people to represent him as talking in these terms afterwards): and although at the time his Good News became no more than a new set of myths (whose meaning is if anything plainer than those of the Old Testament, but which were again firmly locked in theological interpretation), it seems to me that he set currents going in the world which, as I have tried to suggest, eventually brought about a situation in which the myths could indeed break surface and the Good News be proclaimed at last in psychoanalysis.

Freud echoed the essential keynote of the Hebrew/ Christian myths when he spoke, in *Civilization and its Discontents*,[33] of mankind's hope lying in the possibility that eternal *Eros* should put forth new strength against his ancient adversary. What Freud's particular mythological formulation prevented him from seeing was that in his own work, with its emphasis on the liberating power of permissiveness in analysis, this very hope had begun to be realized. If psychoanalysis can now break through to this final insight by unmasking moral sadism as the true age-old adversary of *Eros* and of mankind, there is real hope of our gradually extending the secret of psychoanalytic permissiveness to society as a whole, to create the new kind of community-life which the ancient Hebrew and Christian myths envisage, where the frustration of love is overcome and man begins really to take seriously his power to overcome nature, even the aggressiveness in his own nature. 'The permissive society' is not altogether the best term for this, for it still carries theological overtones of letting other people trample on you because it is morally right, whereas this (as Dr Spock had to insist in the later editions of his famous book) is not what is required at all. What is wanted is a dynamic of human relationships in which each person is prepared to stand up for his own wants without moralizing them, and has *for this very reason* sufficient sensitivity to see that his own fulfilment requires meeting other people as individuals too. The term 'the forgiving society' would be better, but this too carries theological overtones of a different kind, unless it is used by some-one sufficiently well-versed in Blake to know that true forgiveness of sins abolishes any sense that there has been a sin : that was why Blake was able to write

> Mutual forgiveness of each Vice
> ... op'd the gates of Paradise.

and to assert on the other hand that "the punisher alone is the criminal of Providence". I think perhaps the best name for this kind of society towards which we can

now move is the one coined at the turn of the century by
that curious writer Edward Carpenter—a society in
which love has come of age. In so far as anyone achieves
this goal they will be able to appreciate the final truth
that in the end of the day moralism is neither divine nor
even demonic, but merely absurd. As Blake wrote, referring to the Hebrew notion of Satan as the Accuser or
moralizer :

> Truly, My Satan, thou art but a Dunce,
> And dost not know the Garment from the Man.
> Every Harlot was a Virgin once,
> Nor can'st thou ever change Kate into Nan.
> Tho' thou art Worshipp'd by the Names Divine
> Of Jesus and Jehovah, thou art still
> The Son of Morn in weary Night's decline,
> The lost Traveller's Dream under the hill.

Psychoanalysis—Freudian or Existential

PETER LOMAS

I DO not commonly like to regard myself as a Freudian because it implies certain things—that I am an atheist, a pessimist, that I insist that my patients lie on the couch, that I think in terms of id, ego, super-ego, etc.—which, to my mind, are not essential to the practice of psychoanalysis. My only claim to the title is that I have received training at a psychoanalytical institute, that I practise a *technique* of therapy which bears a distinct resemblance to that advocated by Freud, and that I have not discovered any other label to stick on to myself except the generic term 'psychotherapist'. And I hope to imply throughout this essay a condemnation of the type of thinking that freezes people into Freudian, existential, or any other blocks of ice.

Freud grew up intellectually in the philosophical

tradition of late nineteenth-century scientific materialism. It is often forgotten that his first contribution was to neurology—that is to say, it was in the field of physical medicine. When he turned his attention to psychology, he couched his earliest formulations—in his unpublished 'Project' discussed by Ernest Jones[50]—in neurological terminology, and when, later, in *The Interpretation of Dreams*,[21] he proposed the psychological theory that has formed the basis of psychoanalytical thinking, he uses a conceptual framework which markedly resembles the earlier one even though the references to physical structure are no longer there. Freud's failure to emancipate himself from the physical frame of thought has put psychoanalysis into a dilemma of which some practitioners are now becoming aware.

In 1964 Mr H. J. Home read a paper to the British Psycho-analytical Society[45] which began with the passage :

Psychoanalysis began as a study of neurosis and as an hypothesis explaining its origin and development. As an hypothesis about neurosis it might have made little enough stir, in spite of its delineation of an aetiology linking neurosis with sexual frustration, had Freud not invoked a totally new principle of explanation. This principle of explanation, which ran counter to the tenor of thought prevalent in medicine at the time, and which eventually led him on to formulate his revolutionary ideas about the unconscious mind, was that the symptom could have *meaning*.

That the symptom has meaning, if it is neurotic, is Freud's basic discovery, the basic insight which opened up the way to an understanding of functional illness and the principles of psychoanalytic treatment. It is not surprising that, in the excitement of so great a discovery and one that opened up such vast new territories, Freud should have overlooked the logical implications for theory of the step he had taken. Those implications are, however very great, for in the mechanistic medicine of Freud's time, as in all organic medicine of our own day, the symptom is logically regarded as a fact and a fact is regarded as the product of causes. In this, medicine simply follows the practice of chemico-physical science and the canons of thought which are exemplified with special clarity in physics. In discovering that the symptom had meaning and basing his treatment on this hypothesis, Freud took the psychoanalytic study of neurosis out of the world of science into the world of the humanities, because a meaning is not the product of causes but the creation of a subject. This is a major difference; for the logic and method of the humanities is radically different from that of science, though no less respectable and rational and of course much longer established.

The event described by Mr Home has had ironic consequences. The man who, more than any other, has enabled us to see the mentally sick patient as more of a person and less of a thing than had hitherto been possible is now often discredited, especially by existentialists, as a reductionist and a dehumanizer. That this has happened is due to the failure, outside the psychoanalytic movement, to recognize that Freud's findings transcend his language, and, by psychoanalysts themselves, to reformulate his findings in more worthy terms. Mr Home is, alas, the exception and not the rule, and most psychoanalysts do not even recognize the pressing need for such a radical reformulation.

Currently, the psychoanalytic theory which holds the field goes by the name of 'ego psychology' and its leading exponent is Heinz Hartmann.[44] Freud's theory of instinctual drive and his structural model of id, ego and super-ego is retained, but a much greater importance is attached to the ego than before. Psychoanalysts have become concerned with questions about the nature of 'self' and 'identity' and some valuable work has been done, notably by Erik Erikson,[14] in this area of study, but the problem has arisen as to how to bridge the theoretical gap between these new interests and 'ego psychology'. The 'ego' is not the 'self'; it is a construct not an experience, it is mechanistic not personal, and it is alienated from its source of power, the 'id'. Attempts at reconciliation have produced the most ungainly and confused formulations.

What is psychoanalysis to do about this impasse? It is (in America, at least) a social force, it has a well-tried technique (psychoanalysts may adhere to a mechanistic theory, but fortunately they do not practise what they preach, as a perusal of their case-histories will show), and they have a vast clinical literature. Moreover, even confined by a theory that is basically askew, they have produced formulations about mental disharmony which no psychotherapist could ignore without the utmost peril. What must be retained and what should be scrapped? And—relevant to our theme—where does existentialism come in?

Existential analysis, jointly inspired by the work of Freud and the writings of the existentialist philosophers (notably Kierkegaard and Heidegger), had its main authorship in Ludwig Binswanger, a contemporary of Freud's. Much of the writing—and perhaps of the thinking—has not travelled well into Anglo-Saxon countries, although in America Rollo May *et al.* translated key works and elucidated the concepts concerned in their influential book *Existence* in 1958.[68] And the work of Buber and Tillich has made its mark on American psychiatry.

Common to all these thinkers is the basic existential tenet, similar to that expressed by Mr Home in the passage quoted above : the person is more than a thing and cannot be adequately formulated in the terminology of natural science.

Existential analysis, therefore, starts without the encumbrance of a system of psychology based on the physical sciences and views the person as a whole being, the agent of his actions. This does not mean that it has solved the ancient philosophical problem of free will *v.* determinism—or, one of its modern derivatives, the validity of the concept of unconscious thought—but it is a theory which has the pragmatic advantage of being more in accord with our day to day experience of living. The critique which follows has, I hope, some application to the movement as a whole, but I shall confine myself mainly to existentialism in England with which I am most familiar and in sympathy.

The Divided Self

In *The Divided Self*[60] Laing—who, although a trained psychoanalyst, acknowledges his "main intellectual indebtedness to the existential tradition"—uses this approach to criticize conventional psychiatric thinking with the conviction and lucidity unavailable to someone using the theoretical framework of orthodox psychoanalysis (an approach which enables him to make a similar criticism of behaviour therapy).

In a cogent analysis of an interview with a patient

described by Kraepelin (who was primarily responsible for our present classification of mental disorder and who is sometimes referred to as the 'father of modern psychiatry') Laing shows that the psychiatrist is too pre-occupied with categorizing the behaviour of the patient to notice that the 'psychotic' utterances of the latter are reasonable, if disguised, objections to being merely classified and not treated as a person. It is with the dilemma which confronts those who are treated—not only by psychiatrists, but by parents and others—as a thing rather than as a person, and with the schizoid, alienated states which result from such treatment, that Laing is concerned, and, using the existential frame of reference, he is able to present a description of such states more readily comprehensible by, and enriching to, those patients who suffer this particular kind of existence than one given in psychoanalytic terminology.

He writes: "A man may have a sense of his presence in the world as a real, alive, whole, and, in a temporal sense, continuous person. . . . Such a basically *ontologically* secure person will encounter all the hazards of life, social, ethical, spiritual, biological, from a centrally firm sense of his own and other people's reality and identity."

If life-experience has not been such as to enable the person to acquire this "primary ontological security", he is forced into a continuous struggle to maintain a sense of his own being; in this weak position he fears 'engulfment' by others, the 'implosion' of external reality, the 'petrification' of "becoming no more than a thing in the world of the other".

The total self, the 'embodied self', faced with disadvantageous conditions, may split into two parts, a disembodied 'inner self', felt by the person to be the real part of himself, and a 'false self', embodied but dead and futile, which puts up a front of conformity to the world.

Is Laing merely using a more vivid language than that of traditional psychiatry and psychoanalysis or is he producing a more accurate theory of schizoid states? How far has he departed from Freud? What relationship do his ideas have to those of Melanie Klein or Winnicott, two influential British psychoanalysts with whom he has sometimes been compared? An actual problem, interpreted in a Freudian and an existential way, may serve as an introduction to a discussion of the contrasting positions.

In his autobiography *The House of Elrig*,[67] Gavin Maxwell describes two recurrent childhood nightmares "of such dreadful intensity that each was like a death in itself".

In the first dream, "I was playing on the lawn at Tynewood with my sister, the house was behind me, and beyond the lawn was woodland, fringed with rhododendrons. It was a strange half-light, the kind of darkness at noon that may come with a freak thunderstorm or an eclipse of the sun. There were many daisies on the lawn, and I was holding one in my hand when something like the mouth of a gigantic cannon, a vast gaping circle of darkness, ringed with dull metal, loomed out of the trees and grew until there was room for nothing else but it. There was no action, no attempt on my part to escape, only the object itself and the ultimate extreme of fear.

"In the second dream the whole of my vision was filled by a ceiling, an ordinary undecorated ceiling of a pale grey colour. On the surface of this, at the far left and close to the corner, was an object that never came into absolute focus; it appeared to be a short, dark leather strap like a dog collar. Nothing moved; as in the other dream, terror was in the object itself."

Dreams are difficult enough to understand, even when the dreamer is present and can tell us his associations, and I do not propose to attempt a detailed exposition.

A Freudian (or Kleinian) interpretation would focus on anxiety aroused by the instinctual urges, symbolized by items in the dreams, which are of such intensity as to threaten the ego of the child: the thunderstorm may be thought to refer to rage, the gigantic cannon to aggressive—phallic or infantile—'oral' urges. There is certainly, in the first dream, an impressive contrast between the gentle little boy, playing happily with his sister on the lawn, holding a daisy, and the crushing destructiveness of the cannon. Such contrasts are typical of the conflict between aggressive impulse and the 'reaction formation' against it.

But what of the circumstances of the dreams? Maxwell tells us that they reached their climax during his internment in a preparatory boarding school, a school passionately dedicated to the suppression of individuality in its pupils, the emotional atmosphere of which was even more chilling than the early morning cold showers which were a routine feature of the curriculum.

Shortly before this climax was reached Maxwell was admonished for using his own portable inkwell by a senior boy: "You've got to learn to be like other people." His subsequent attempt to assert his individuality in this matter failed ignominiously.

If one turns again to the dreams one can see that they both depict a situation of paralysis in the face of a crushing environment; the images—an "eclipse of the sun", a "vast gaping darkness, ringed with dull metal ...grew until there was room for nothing else but it", a grey ceiling, a dog collar—these are images of constriction and oppression. The dreams depict, in fact, the actual situation of the boy, and it is upon this aspect that an existential approach would focus: the present predicament of the person (as a whole) in his immediate interpersonal relationships in the school—and also with his family who were responsible for sending him to the school.

These dreams were not analysed, the services of no therapist were called upon, but the boy was cured—or rather, cured himself. Presumably because he retained sufficient belief in himself, in life, or in his mother's capacity to respond to an extreme appeal, he took desperate action which resulted in his removal from the school. Once removed, his peace of mind was restored and he prospered.

It would appear, therefore, that the second, existential kind of interpretation of the dream is the more meaningful. It does not follow, however, that the first view is incorrect, or the second comprehensive. As Freud has shown, dreams are massively condensed structures. There is plenty of biographical evidence in Maxwell's book to suggest the existence of serious sexual and aggressive repression at the time of the dreams.

Melanie Klein

Melanie Klein[56] [57] [58] has made an enormous impression on the theory and practice of psychoanalysis in this country. Basing her ideas on child analysis—of which she was a pioneer—she held that the crucial period of life was infancy and that the innate aggressive tendencies of the baby led him early into intolerable conflict over love and hate from which he tried to escape by projecting the aggressive part of himself on to the outer world.

Like Freud, she emphasized the disrupting effect of powerful instinctual drive, but she focused on the aggressive rather than the sexual drive and believed that the major conflict occurred at even an earlier age than did he. Although all of us, she held, carry the scars of this struggle, those destined to become 'schizoid' have been crippled by it.

The anxieties characteristic of the schizoid person, described by Laing as "ontological insecurity", "a fear of engulfment", etc. are discussed by Melanie Klein in terms of "persecutory anxiety", "projective and introjective identification", but the similarity of descriptive clinical detail is apparent. Both writers are impressed by the splitting mechanisms which occur, on feelings of inner deadness and impoverishment, on terror of an invasion into the very core of the self. But the agreement ends here. Laing believes that such a person is struggling to maintain his sense of identity in the face of a total life-experience designed to destroy it. Melanie Klein held the view that such insecurity arises from unrealistic fantasies of attack which in turn have their source in the person's projection of his aggression; this projection takes place in infancy in cases where there is an excess of aggression either innately determined or engendered by physical frustration, and is therefore experienced in terms of bodily fantasy, the mouth and breast having special significance.

Having myself[63] come to view the nature of fears of 'engulfment' in a way rather similar to that of Laing, I must confess to a leaning towards his explanation and language. Melanie Klein, in fact, is no existentialist, but a true Freudian, deeply committed to instinct theory, almost blind to the life circumstances of the patient. Although she tried to develop a theory of interpersonal relationships (which, in psychoanalytical theory goes by the unfortunate term "*object* relationships") she did not achieve the success of Fairbairn[18] in this venture. Persons do not, in her thinking, ever really emerge from their internal fantasy world; love is not a spontaneous emotion but is based on a need to make reparation for aggressive wishes and fantasies. Her contribution lies not in basic theory but in her description of certain defence mechanisms. She has, for instance, extended our awareness of projection, revealing that not only aggression is projected but also other undesirable states of mind such as anxiety, guilt and depression, and that such projection is often accompanied by a massive identification, depleting to the self. That her work provoked such a furore within the psychoanalytic movement is surprising in view of its intrinsic significance, and is to be attributed to a combination of group intolerance and her own tendency to write somewhat dogmatically.

The difference between the Freudian and the existential point of view is therefore not bridged in any way by the work of Melanie Klein, for her position is essentially that of Freud. But this difference is not one of total incompatibility; there is no reason why both the intrusion of the environment and the projection of undesired emotional states should not combine in the production of symptoms. About the language used to describe the experiences of engulfment, etc., a further point needs to be added. If the schizoid person is encouraged—as he is by Laing—to formulate his anxieties in non-bodily, non-infantile language, may this not facilitate the idealization of conceptual thinking at the expense of bodily experience to which the schizoid person is rather prone? Is there not a danger of forgetting that the original deprivations, even if best formulated in terms of 'self', 'identity' and so on, were to a large extent physical? However misguided was Freud's biological theory of human development it enabled him to remain aware at all times that we have bodies.

Winnicott

Like Melanie Klein, Winnicott derived many of his ideas from the psychoanalysis of children, but is more concerned than she with the actuality of the mother-baby relationship. He believes that it is a failure on the part of the mother to make meaningful contact with her baby that prevents him from revealing his 'true self' to her and forces him into a schizoid mould in which a 'false self' is presented to the world, leaving the 'true self' buried and unmanifest. The similarity of language to that of Laing in describing this alienated condition is clear, yet Winnicott does not appear to claim any kinship with the existential tradition.

Although much of Winnicott's thought stems from his work with mothers and babies, the paper in which he describes his theory of schizoid states is based on his observation of adult patients in the psychoanalytic setting.[85] His experience led him to believe that for certain patients it is necessary, at some point in the analysis, to give up a 'false' independence and regress to a state of 'real' dependence on the analyst, who may, at this stage, be called upon to 'hold' the patient in addition to performing his customary function of interpretation. If the outcome of this crisis is satisfactory the patient begins to trust the outer world; his 'true self' may then emerge, and grow.

In this conception the inner self is not only felt as more real by the patient but contains the germ of the 'true self,' 'frozen' at the time of the environmental failure, waiting to be awakened by a kinder world. The 'false self' not only conforms, in the meaningless way described by Laing, to the demands of the outer world, but acts as a 'caretaker' to the 'true self'. Apart from the fact that Winnicott is concerned with a therapeutic technique rather than a clinical or theoretical description of schizoid states, the main difference in his approach is his belief in the existence of a pre-split 'real' self to which one has to return. Like Laing, Winnicott focuses on the 'impingement' of a disruptive environment on a vulnerable self, but he places the critical time for this occurrence in infancy. He believes, as did Freud, that it is necessary in therapy to revive an early infantile memory. This does not mean that particular well-defined incidents need emerge from repression, but that there must be a return to the infantile experience of simple, passionate openness preceding the disappointment that led to withdrawal and splitting. Certain elements in Winnicott's terminology remain unsatisfactory, for he has tried to retain Freudian 'metapsychology' in parts of his description, and a clear distinction between the pre-split self, the 'false self', and the distorted fantasy-system of the 'inner self' is lacking, but he conveys, even more vividly than Laing, the picture of a self that remains its own agent in any eventuality and however disguised, and he retains the conception—vital to psychoanalytic thought—of a return to the past. This last factor is of crucial importance in any discussion of the different viewpoints of Freudian and existential analysis.

The 'Unconscious'

One of the cornerstones of Freud's theory is 'unconsciousness', a concept closely linked to 'repression' (of thoughts and feelings into the unconscious), to the

'transference' (of unconscious—particularly infantile—
yearnings on to the analyst) and 'resistance' (to acceptance of the emergent wishes and fears).

Existentialists are keenly critical about this concept.
Sartre, in *Being and Nothingness*[75] demonstrates that
the notion of 'unconsciousness' is in fact a contradiction
in terms.

A distinction must be made here between disagreements about the *concept* of 'the unconscious' and about
the nature of that which the term denotes. As regards
the former, one may accept that Freud's formulation of
'the unconscious' is unsatisfactory inasmuch as it gives
the impression of an actual place in the mind into which
things could be put. But there is no objection, except
perhaps a semantic one, to his use of the term when
describing certain experiences in psychoanalytic treatment (a fact which some existentialists, including Laing,
accept). The illumination that occurs when a potential
perception is made actual is an experience of everyday
life carrying conviction, although seldom felt with the
intensity with which it occurs in a psychotherapeutic
setting. It would seem likely that an explanation of what
makes it impossible to actualize a potential experience
awaits resolution of the question as to what makes it
possible. In the meantime we need the term (or some
equivalent) just as we need the term 'free will' (or
'agency'), for which also there is no adequate conception.

Given this amount of agreement, there would appear
to be no reason why existentialists should object to the
concept of 'transference' of unconscious material on to
the analyst, yet this concept is little mentioned in existential writings. The reason for this, I suspect, is partly
a disagreement with Freud as to what is transferred,

and partly the fear of an unhealthy preoccupation with the past.

In psychoanalytical theory, what is transferred to the analyst is infantile urge; the past is reconstructed and old conflicts can be understood and resolved. But, due to the way in which this theory has been formulated, and because of their (natural) concern to avoid undue focus on past, rather than present and future, issues, existentialists remain wary of the concept.

Assuming that—to continue to use Freudian terminology—certain factors in the personality can be rendered unconscious (repressed) in a way that is harmful to the person, what are these factors? It is here, I think, that the main disagreement lies. Freud considered them to be derived from libidinal and aggressive instinctual urges. The Existentialist would, I assume, regard them as representations of the authentic self, although preferring the term 'alienation' to 'repression'.

However, if it is recognized, by both schools of thought, that what are transferred to the analyst are primarily those urges of the self that have been denied expression, and that the authentic self is concerned not merely with past frustrations but with present and future possibilities of relationship, there would appear to be no inevitable reason for disagreement over this question.

The 'True' and the 'False' Self

The artist may be famed for the actual piece of work that he does, but the scientist who seeks distinction must discover a new thing or conceive a new law. In the field of psychoanalysis, where there is no firmly established language except that of Freud, in which to describe the phenomena, those workers with personal ambition fall into the temptation of providing new verbal formulations, and this is perhaps one of the reasons for the existence of a superfluity of verbal concepts. It is important, therefore, to view any new terminology with circumspection. However, the distinction between the true (real) and the false self has two important merits: it is immediately meaningful in terms of human experience and it has arisen independently in the minds of several thinkers. But is it a distinction which will really enrich our theory of personality? Does it describe anything which the traditional psychoanalytic theory cannot?

Much, in fact, that is denoted by the word 'false' can be adequately accounted for by Freud's term 'defensive.' A 'defence' is a manoeuver to prevent the expression of an 'instinctual' impulse considered likely, for one reason or another, to have undesirable effects in life. The impulse in question will then be repressed (or suffer some other vicissitude such as projection), with the consequence that actual behaviour will no longer be a relatively accurate expression of personality but will give a false, disguised and distorted picture of it. A person who, for instance, has repressed viciousness may present a mild and equable demeanour. In terms of the dichotomy under consideration his 'instinctive' self is the true one, his defences and their consequences false. But suppose that his viciousness is not primary but is itself merely a disguise or a relatively meaningless escape valve? Does one not again have to put the question: "Is his behaviour true or false?" And does not the Freudian theory become at this point—to say the least—unnecessarily complicated? Why did not Freud formulate his ideas in terms of trueness or authenticity? Chiefly, it would seem, because he used the biological framework. But there is, perhaps, another reason.

Freud's theory of human growth appears to be one of continuity: he has spelled out the ways in which the child is father to the man, the degree to which we carry our childhood with us; and, indeed, is often criticised for dwelling too much on ontological development. Yet he regarded growth less as a continuing evolution than as a gradual *victory* of each stage over the past; the 'pleasure principle' must succumb to the 'reality principle'; each new self discards the old, even if traces of it remain to harass and embarrass. Freud is here caught between the authenticity of the past and of the present, and his thinking does not allow for the unfolding of a true self which remains intact as the core of personality, a unique entity gathering meaning as it grows, discarding only those aims and illusions that are peripheral to its being, whose quality is measured not by stage of development, degree of libidinization, or physical mode of expression, but by its experienced meaningfulness and manifest spontaneity. In a theory of continuity the main dichotomy is not between past and present or id and ego but between what is true and what is false.

Is it possible to reformulate Freud's theory—which can account, so nearly adequately, for so much—in these sort of terms without losing more than is gained?

A first move would seem to be the acceptance of Fairbairn's view[18] that the infant starts life in an integrated, 'pristine' state which dissociates only in the face of adverse circumstances, and to equate this state with that of the true self, which is spontaneous, concerned with meaning and the agent of its own action. The integration is primary but not absolute, in that certain determinants of behaviour—such as reflex actions—have their own relative independence. These elements constitute behaviour which in animal life is called 'instinctual', but it does not follow that the spontaneous urge of the true self lacks biological foundation.

In the imperfect world in which the true self finds itself it inevitably becomes modified in a way that fails to do justice to its potential. At what point does the distortion of the original urge become so marked as to justify the view that a 'false self' is operating? The answer to this would appear to be somewhat arbitrary, depending on whether one is an idealist or a cynic, and is equivalent to the vexed question which occurs in traditional psychoanalytical thought: "When is behaviour 'adaptive' and when 'defensive'?" But it would perhaps be least confusing to restrict the term 'false' to behaviour designed, for whatever reason, to conceal the existence of the true self and therefore to deny meaning. The reasons for this kind of aim would include the avoidance of a real experience of life that was too awful to contemplate, the preservation (as Winnicott has shown) of a hidden but intact true self, and the attainment of some kind of meaning and satisfaction from the spurious personality which is erected. Although some satisfaction may be gained in this way, true meaning cannot. In such a state the person is 'depersonalized'; his identity is based on delusion and parasitism, dependent on the use of mechanisms known to psychoanalysts by such terms as introjection, identification, narcissism, masochism, etc.; he has become a quisling, and has, in Anna Freud's phrase, "identified with the aggressor", the latter being, in this context, the world which has prevented him from becoming himself. This kind of aim includes, but is much more extensive than, that covered by Freud's conception of the "secondary gain of illness".

Actual behaviour will necessarily be a function of both the true and the false. The person who has—if only temporarily—abandoned his main spontaneous urge to living will attempt to express it in whatever manner, however limited, that remains open to him. In his restricted state he may, if fortunate, find surprising yet creative ways of revealing his true self, as in the symbolism of art, but it is likelier—because easier—that he be more able to give vent to, in distorted form, the destructive aspects of his real response to experience.

Any alteration in basic theoretical orientation will have an effect on clinical practice and on the way in which particular clinical states are formulated. What difference would be made by the change in emphasis under discussion? One might expect, for instance, that a psychoanalyst thinking in this kind of framework would focus on the authenticity of a piece of behaviour; that, for instance, he would be quick to consider whether the aggression of a paranoid patient was an attempt to ward off engulfment (being an expression of the true self) or was a *pretence* of aggression in order to give the impression that no such fear existed. Psychoanalysts do, of course, seek out such distinctions, but their present theoretical framework does not readily give them the mental set for such a task.

Hysteria

The division into true and false has so far been used in this essay, in considering schizoid states. Can it be applied to other clinical conditions? Let us take hysteria as an example.

According to current psychoanalytic theory, hysterical

symptoms occur when an instinctive (usually sexual) urge is repressed and appears in symbolic form in an unexpected area of experience. For instance, a woman may repress a sexual impulse only to find herself plagued by a disturbance of swallowing; analysis reveals that, unconsciously, vaginal sensations have been displaced on to the mouth and pharynx. This kind of event (though usually in a much more complicated form than the example given) has frequently been described in the psychoanalytic literature, but is it sufficient to account for the main characteristic of hysteria: dramatization? It is a fact that the hysteric is acting a part in a play which exists in the realm of unconscious fantasy, but so are many people who lack the distinctive excitability and flair of the hysteric. Classical theory attempts to deal with this by the concept of 'hysterical character': whole areas of experience are 'libidinized', giving an orgastic quality to behaviour. But this in turn is unsatisfactory. The behaviour in question is not merely orgastic (and is not usually resolved by giving it this interpretation) but has a quality of pseudo-liveliness about it, as though the woman were trying to convince herself and others that she is alive, and very much so. And such a woman may well be having perfectly good orgasms all the time; the important question is whether her sexuality—and her behaviour in general—is true or false.

The idea that the dramatization of hysteria derives from a false self would seem to account for it more easily and more adequately than does the present theory. One is reminded of the little girl described by Winnicott[86] who was gay and who danced beautifully to offset her mother's depression, and of the patients described by Melanie Klein as manifesting a 'manic defence' against depression. (There is a greater similarity between mania and hysteria than is easily accounted for). The hysteric who so pitifully tries to present herself as real, lively and desirable does so, perhaps, because her true self has been repressed; she feels an empty shell, yet those around expect vitality. An important differentiating factor in the aetiology of the false self of the schizoid and that of the hysteric may lie in the kind of personality demanded by the family into which he or she is born.

Inasmuch, then, as hysterical behaviour is false, the current psychodynamic theory is called into question, for the symptoms are less a distorted expression of the primary drive than a meaningless substitute for it. Freud has described the way in which a drive and its defence can be skilfully woven into a compromise symptom, and the primary drive no doubt reveals itself, when possible, even in the spurious activities of the hysteric; but it is likely that the real feelings which emerge are mainly aggressive ones and that much at present considered true (even if distorted) is really false. This would account for the fact that hysteria is a much more difficult condition to treat than would be expected if Freud's theory of it were quite correct. That sexuality plays such a central role in the condition may be due not merely to the fact that sexuality is one of the things which are repressed but that it is a suitable and powerful symbol of liveliness; and women may suffer from the disease more frequently than men because they get more encouragement, in our culture, to be false to themselves.

Psychic Economy

Although Freud understood his patients by discovering the meaning of their symptoms, his theory of personality is based on psychic economy—the distribution of energy within the mind. If one is to consider the possibility of developing a theory of mind based on the consequences of meaningful action where, if at all, does psychic economy play a part?

Even when discussing healthy, spontaneous behaviour we cannot, in fact, entirely disregard the question of psychic energy, for it is bound to influence our choice of action. I may wish to finish this essay at one sitting but I know that eventually, through mental fatigue, I would either have to stop or else severely limit my goal; and I think this would be true at a certain point even in the absence of neurotic inhibition.

In pathological states, however, psychic economy may restrict choice much more ruthlessly and perhaps even dictate the scene. So much energy may be lost through repression and dissociation or locked in the vicious circles of obsessional thinking that there is little left for the ordinary task of living. Moreover, the available energy may be of a different quality from the natural one, or forced to operate in a different way. When dissociation occurs—as it does in all mental ill-health—it is likely that energy takes on a cruder form; in the same way, perhaps, that there is a release of crude neuronal discharge from the brain stem when the cortex is put out of action. This could account, at least in part, for some of the clinical states associated with 'primitive' behaviour: urgency, impatience, anxiety, greed, rigidity, and so on.

A distinction of this kind between refined (integrated) and crude (disintegrated) energy brings to mind Freud's differentiation between the "unbound" energy of the "id" and the "bound" energy of the "ego". Are they equivalent? In considering unbound energy to be primitive, Freud believed that it partook of the nature of the child, and it is possible that he was somewhat mistaken in this, underestimating the child's degree of integration and capacity for personal experience. (That he was —at least to a degree—is suggested by the work of Schachtel[76] on infant development and by Rycroft[74] on the activity of the "id" and the "ego".) If this is so, Freud is attributing a kind of normality (even if ontogenetically regressed) to this crude activity which it does not really possess, with the consequence that he may have seen meaning in it which is not there.

This line of thought has led to a paradoxical idea: that Freud, who (as I indicated at the beginning of this essay) seems to need to be defended against the accusation that his approach is too mechanistic, sees meaning where he should be seeing mechanism, i.e. the inevitable consequences of psychic dissociation which are quite outside the scope of the person's will, regardless of whether the latter is considered to be conscious or unconscious. If he has done this, then psychoanalysts have followed him—and gone further. Very few clinical psychoanalytic studies—Federn[19] being a brilliant exception—take much account of psychic economy. Melanie Klein, for instance, writes as though the correct therapeutic response to every psychopathological state is an interpretation.

Because the great contribution of psychoanalysis has been to understand the meaning of symptoms, the fact that they may have overestimated the territory in which this is possible is perhaps inevitable and of secondary importance. But the error needs to be recognized for the sake of theory and practice. To know when a patient is so trapped by his psychic economy that he cannot, however willing, respond to interpretations, may be crucial, and a mistake of this kind is so painful to the patient that he may not easily forgive the analyst for making it. It is perhaps here that Winnicott's concept of "holding" the patient in certain critical states of mind is appropriate. Another reason for mistakenly attributing meaning to a symptom is the natural fear which the psychoanalyst has of colluding with the patient's passive urge to renounce responsibility for his actions, an urge that is so widespread in our culture that Szasz[80] considers it to be the key to mental illness. Szasz is stimulating and in many ways convincing on this subject but it would seem that, like the existentialists (who ignore psychic economy completely), he overstates a valid and valuable case.

Schizophrenia and the Family

In their recent book *Sanity, Madness and the Family*[62] —the first volume of a series—Laing and Esterson describe a study of families, one of whose members had been diagnosed by psychiatrists as schizophrenic. A notable feature of the recorded interviews is that little interpretation was made and the family was permitted to reveal itself with a minimum of interference.

Contrary to the expectations of current psychiatric thought, the authors found that the 'patient' presented a view of events, which, in their estimation, was often nearer the truth than that of the rest of the family. When she (the study was confined to female schizophrenics) revealed 'delusions' of persecution she was describing, in unusual and picturesque language, what was actually being done to her by the family at a certain level of experience. Her identity was being crushed because the family colluded, in cruel and subtle ways, in invalidating her experience of life, causing her to doubt the evidence of her senses. We are made to feel how, if we had been put in the same position as the 'victim', we would have been hard pressed to find a better solution than she did.

These findings suggest to the authors that schizophrenia is not, as is commonly thought, a disease process, but the label attached to a type of behaviour shown by certain people who, having been subjected to strange experiences by their families, come, understandably, to behave in a strange way themselves. If this finding is correct—and the book is, by and large, convincing—it constitutes a very powerful opposition to the traditional psychiatric theory of the origin of schizophrenia, and, by demonstrating that pathogenic influences are being exerted by the family in the *present*, it challenges the psychoanalytic theory that schizophrenia originates in a faulty mother–infant set-up. Recently Dr David Cooper[9] has described an experimental approach to the organization of a mental hospital ward based on ideas similar to those presented by Laing and Esterson.

This approach to schizophrenic families is not exclusive to the British existentialist school of thought, for much work has been done on these lines in America, but it would seem that their conception of personality has helped the authors to explore very fruitfully the schizophrenic's search for identity and the truth in his apparently mad perceptions. One criticism which a psychoanalyst would make of their formulations, however favourable he might be to the work, is that the events are being described as though the "patient" were contributing nothing to the disaster. The psychoanalysis of schizophrenia has shown that the pathological distortions of love and hate characteristic of this illness, engendered by whatever original causes, are self-destructive and involve a masochistic manipulation of others to behave badly towards the self. It is difficult to believe that this tendency does not contribute in some measure to the clinical picture described by Laing and Esterson, and a more likely assumption to make is that an early parent–child failure has been followed by a vicious circle in which both family and victim play their unhappy parts.

If this is correct, then the authors have shown a bias in which aggressive action is attributed to the parents (and siblings) alone. In one sense this is natural enough, for the authors are coming to the aid of someone whose voice has been unheard for too long. But perhaps there is more to it than this. Theoretical preoccupations tend to make workers selective in their perception of clinical phenomena, and in concentrating on the reality concealed in the patient's perception of others they may have overlooked some indirect methods of action used by him to express his identity. There is a possibility that the existentialists, although usefully emphasizing the agency of the person, may—paradoxically—by denying the validity of what psychoanalysts refer to as "unconscious motivation" or "repressed drive", fail to see the agency of the person in certain pathological techniques.

Personal Relationships

In spite of the fact that he revealed much about human relationships, Freud was more concerned with intrapsychic phenomena and his theory reflected this preoccupation; nor has psychoanalysis been successful hitherto in finding a framework within which to describe what actually occurs between persons. This is a field in which one would expect the existentialists, who are concerned with 'Being-in-the-World' to have made some advance. How successful have they been?

In his article, 'Two Types of Rationality',[10] Dr
David Cooper criticizes "analytical rationality"—the
traditional logic of human relationships in which truth
is considered to lie outside the reality of the relationship,
the observer and observed being in passive relationship
with each other. By contrast:

> Human reality is that sector of reality where totaliza-
> tion is the very mode of being. A totality is something
> completed which therefore can be grasped as a whole;
> a totalization, on the other hand, is a perpetual move-
> ment... What goes on in the reciprocal relation of a
> two-person transaction is as follows: I totalize you,
> but you, in your reciprocal totalization of me, include
> my totalization of you, so that my totalization of you
> involves a totalization of your totalization of me, and
> so on....

This view of human relations was anticipated by
Sartre in his earlier work, *Being and Nothingness*, in
a familiar example:[75]

> "I am surreptitiously looking through a keyhole at a
> scene in the next room. I become aware of a presence
> behind me. I turn and discover that someone has been
> watching me. At that moment a 'haemorrhage'
> occurs. The pure subjectivity that I have been exist-
> ing as an observer of the scene in the next room drains
> away from my world into the world of the other
> where I become nothing more than a shameful object
> observed by him. At least until I find a way to regain
> my existence, return to the centre of *my* world and
> reduce the other in turn to being an object for me."

This little example is evidently intended to convey
what is typical of human relationships in general, yet the
impression actually given is of a particular kind of

relationship, one in which the two people are either unknown to each other, or, if known, do not possess a sense of mutual trust and affection. There is an assumption that the first person (at the keyhole) deeply minds the unexpected observation of the second, will necessarily cringe before his glance, and that his only mode of recovering his sense of dignity and identity is by retaliatory observation. There would appear to be no possibility, in this formulation of the scene, that a relationship might exist between the two people that is characterized by love and which transcends or precludes the shame and disintegration. Or that, if shame occurs, that it might be followed by acceptance and growth rather than retaliation. (I do not mean to imply that I believe in the existence of relationships so ideal that the participants do not sometimes act in a retaliatory way upon each other, but that it is a mistake to assume it to be the natural, inevitable reaction.)

The type of relationship formulated by Cooper would seem to be one in which elements of control, manipulation and narcissistic assertion are uppermost; the conception of an atmosphere of love, trust, defencelessness, contemplation is lacking. Once again there is a paradox. The psychology that is attempting to describe the possibilities of human freedom finds itself not necessarily more successful in the attempt than those before it.

In *The Self and Others*,[61] Laing uses the terminology of "person perception psychology", a phenomenological approach, developed by Heider and others, to describe human relationships, in which the implicit attributions people make about each other are carefully analysed. The usefulness of this language, however, remains in doubt; it shows signs of becoming lost in mathematical formulae, a fate which befell the promising work of Kurt Lewin.

Laing is a perceptive clinician and a vigorous and creative thinker who makes use of whatever bits of language he can lay his hands on, and for this reason *The Self and Others* is a rewarding book. It does not follow from this that the Heiderian terminology is entirely safe as a basis for a study of relationships. There is a dilemma in that all descriptions of human behaviour that depart from ordinary language are in danger of leading us into the very kind of arid, atomistic, mechanistic world which the existentialists are so anxious to avoid. The need for a satisfactory language with which to discuss relationships in a scientific way is a pressing one and has not yet been met.

Existentialism and Psychoanalysis

Existentialism has a theoretical orientation more suited to the study of persons than has that of psychoanalysis. In this country its exponents are characterized by a preoccupation with schizophrenia, a tendency to support the underdog, a leaning towards the philosophy of Sartre—and courage—and have already made some useful contributions to an understanding of schizoid states and, especially, of the relationships within a family containing a schizophrenic member.

The potential of this new approach is limited, at present, by the fact that some fruitful channels opened by psychoanalysis are being neglected. Can the existentialists afford to put aside the technique of 'transference' interpretation? To what degree does their work suffer if they do not take into consideration the two types of symbolic thinking described by Freud as "primary process" (typified by dreams) and "secondary process" (typified by conscious logic)? Have they paid sufficient attention to guilt, mourning and depression, to psychic economy, to child development, or to the fact that there are two sexes involved in human intercourse?

Psychotherapy constitutes the only real challenge and alternative to the barren, organic school of psychiatry that holds sway in our country, and its practitioners cannot afford to be catastrophically divided among themselves. It would be a great pity if the 'Freudian' and 'existential' schools of thought grew apart rather than together.

This essay has been enlarged from an article first published in Views, Summer 1965.

Bibliography

1. ALEXANDER, F. *and* FRENCH, T. M. *Psychoanalytic therapy.* New York, Ronald Press, 1946.

2. BACHELARD, Gaston. *The psychoanalysis of fire.* Translated by A. C. M. Ross. Boston, Beacon Press, 1964.

3. BAILEY, Derrick S. *Man-woman relation in Christian thought.* London, Longmans, Green, 1959.

4. BIRNEY, R. C. *and* TEEVAN, R. C. *eds. Instinct,* Princeton, N.J., Insight Books (Van Nostrand), 1961.

5. BONAPARTE, Marie. *The life and works of Edgar Allen Poe.* Translated by J. Rodker. New York, Hillary House, 1965.

6a. BOWLBY, John. An ethological approach to research in child development. *Brit. J. Med. Psychol.* 1957, *30,* 230–40.

6b. BOWLBY, John. The nature of the child's tie to his mother. *Int. J. Psycho-Anal.* 1958, *39,* 350–373.

7. BUYTENDIJCK, F. J. J. *Pain: its modes and functions.* Translated by E. O'Shiel. Chicago, Univ. of Chicago Press, 1966.

8. CARTHY, J. D. *and* EBLING, F. J. *eds. The natural history of aggression.* New York & London, Academic Press, 1964.

9. COOPER, David. 'The anti-hospital: an experiment in psychiatry.' *New Society*, 11th March 1965, 5, No. 128.

10. COOPER, David. 'Two types of rationality.' *New Left Review*, Jan.–Feb. 1965, No. 29, 62–68.

11. ERICKSON, E. H. 'Observations on the Yurok: childhood and world image.' *Univ. Calif. Publ. Amer. Archaeol. Ethn.*, 1943, *35*, No. 10, 257–302.

12. ERIKSON, E. H. 'Childhood and tradition in two American Indian tribes.' *Psychoanal. Stud. Child*, 1945, *1*, 319–350.

13. ERIKSON, E. H. *Young man Luther.* New York, Norton, 1958.

14. ERIKSON, E. H. 'Identity and the life cycle.' *Psychol. Issues*, 1959, *1*, No. 1.

15. ERIKSON, E. H. *Childhood and society.* 2nd edition. New York, Norton, 1963.

16. EYSENCK, H. J. *The uses and abuses of psychology.* New York, Penquin Books, 1953.

Bibliography

17. EYSENCK, H. J. *Fact and fiction in psychology.* New York, Penguin Books, 1965.

18. FAIRBAIRN, W. R. D. *Psychoanalytic studies of the personality.* London, Tavistock Publications, 1952.

19. FEDERN, Paul. *Ego psychology and the psychoses.* New York, Basic Books, 1953.

20. FORDHAM, Michael. *The objective psyche.* New York, Humanities Press, 1958.

21. FREUD, Sigmund. *The interpretation of dreams.* New York, Basic Books, 1955.

22. FREUD, Sigmund. *Jokes and their relation to the unconscious.* New York, Norton, 1960.

23. FREUD, Sigmund. *The antithetical meaning of primal words.* 1910. Standard edition, vol. II. London, Hogarth Press, 1957.

24. FREUD, Sigmund. *Totem and taboo.* New York, Norton, 1952.

25. FREUD, Sigmund. *The Moses of Michelangelo.* (1914). Standard edition, vol. 13. London, Hogarth Press, 1955.

26. FREUD, Sigmund. *Papers on metapsychology.* (1915). Standard edition, vol. 14. London, Hogarth Press, 1957.

27. FREUD, Sigmund. *Introductory lectures on psychoanalysis.* (1916–1917). Lecture 6. Standard edition, vol. 15. London, Hogarth Press, 1963.

28. FREUD, Sigmund. *Introductory lectures on psychoanalysis.* (1916–1917). Lecture 17. Standard edition, vol. 16. London, Hogarth Press, 1963.

29. FREUD, Sigmund. *From the history of an infantile neurosis.* (1918). Standard edition, vol. 17. London, Hogarth Press, 1955.

30. FREUD, Sigmund. *Beyond the pleasure principle.* New York, Liveright.

31. FREUD, Sigmund. *A seventeenth century demonological neurosis.* (1923). *In* Standard Edition, vol. 19. London, Hogarth Press, 1961.

32. FREUD, Sigmund. *The future of an illusion.* New York, Liveright.

33. FREUD, Sigmund. *Civilization and its discontents.* (1930). Standard edition, vol. 21. London, Hogarth Press, 1961.

34. FREUD, Sigmund. *Moses and monotheism.* New York, Vintage, 1955.

35. FREUD, Sigmund. *An outline of psychoanalysis.* New York, Norton, 1949.

36. FROMM, Erich. *The Forgotten Language.* New York, Holt, Rinehart & Winston, 1951.

37. FROMM, Erich. *The sane society.* New York, Holt, Rinehart & Winston, 1956.

38. GORER, Geoffrey. *The Americans.* London, Cresset Press, 1948.

39. GORER, Geoffrey. *Exploring English Character.* New York, S. G. Phillips, 1955.

40. GRODDECK, Georg. *The book of the It.* Translated by M. E. Collins. New York, Vintage.

41. GUNTRIP, Harry. *Personality-structure and human interaction.* New York, International Universities, 1964.

42. GUTKIND, Erich. *The absolute collective.* Rochford, Essex, C. W. Daniel, 1937.

43. HARTMANN, Heinz. *Ego psychology and the problem of adaptation.* New York, International Universities Press, 1958.

44. HARTMANN, Heinz. *Essays on ego psychology.* New York, International Universities Press, 1964.

45. HOME, H. J. 'The concept of mind.' *Int. J. Psychoanal.*, 1966, *47*, 42–49.

46. HORNEY, Karen. *The neurotic personality of our time.* New York, Norton, 1937.

47. HORNEY, Karen. *New ways in psychoanalysis.* New York, Norton, 1939.

48. HORNEY, Karen. *Our inner conflicts.* New York, Norton, 1945.

49. JONES, Ernest. *Hamlet and Oedipus.* New York, Doubleday, 1954.

50. JONES, Ernest. *Sigmund Freud: Life and Work. Vol. I.* New York, Basic Books, 1953.

51. JUNG, Carl G. *Modern man in search of a soul.* New York, Harcourt, Brace, 1933.

52. JUNG, Carl G. *Two essays on analytical psychology.* New York, Meridian Books, 1956.

53. JUNG, Carl G. *Psychology and religion: west and east.* New Haven, Yale University Press, 1938.

54. JUNG, Carl G. *The archetypes and the collective unconscious.* Collected works, vol. 9, part I. New York, Pantheon, 1959.

55. JUNG, Carl G. *Memories, dreams and reflections.* Edited by A. Jaffé. New York, Pantheon, 1963.

56. KLEIN, Melanie. *Contributions to psychoanalysis, 1921–1945.* New York, Hillary House, 1948.

57. KLEIN, Melanie. *The psychoanalysis of children.* 3rd edition. New York, Hillary House, 1932.

58. KLEIN, Melanie. *et al. Developments in psychoanalysis.* New York, Hillary House, 1936.

59. KOESTLER, Arthur. *The act of creation.* New York, Macmillan, 1964.

60. LAING, R. D. *The Divided self.* New York, Penguin Books, 1965.

61. LAING, R. D. *The self and others.* London, Tavistock Publications, 1961.

62. LAING, R. D. *and* ESTERSON, A. *Sanity, madness and family.* Vol I: Families of schizophrenics. New York, Basic Books, 1965.

63. LOMAS, Peter, 'Family role and identity formation.' *Int. J. Psycho-Anal.*, 1961, *42*, 371–380.

64. LONDON, P. *The modes and morals of psychotherapy.* New York, Holt, Rinehart & Winston, 1964.

65. LORENZ, Konrad. *King Solomon's ring.* New York, Crowell, 1962.

66. MACMURRAY, John. *Persons in relation.* New York, Humanities Press, 1961.

67. MAXWELL, Gavin. *The house of Elrig.* New York, Dutton, 1965.

68. MAY, Rollo. *et al., eds. Existence.* New York, Basic Books, 1958.

69. MONEY-KYRLE, R. *Psychoanalysis and politics.* London, Duckworth, 1951.

70. NEWSON, J. *and* NEWSON, E. *Patterns of infant care in an urban community.* New York, Penguin Books, 1965.

71. ORWELL, George. *Nineteen eighty-four.* New York, Harcourt, Brace, 1949.

72. RóHEIM, Géza. *Psychoanalysis and anthropology.* New York, International Universities Press, 1950.

73. RUSSELL, Bertrand. 'A Free man's worship.' In *Mysticism and logic*. New York, Barnes & Noble, 1954.

74. RYCROFT, Charles. 'Beyond the reality principle.' *Int. J. Psycho-Anal.*, 1962, *43*, 388–394.

75. SARTRE, J. P. *Being and nothingness*. Translated by H. E. Barnes. New York, Citadel, 1964.

76. SCHACHTEL, Ernest G. *Metamorphosis*. New York, Basic Books, 1959.

77. SHARPE, Ella F. *Collected papers on psychoanalysis*. Edited by M. Brierley. London, Hogarth Press, 1950.

78. SHELDON, William H. *Varieties of delinquent youth*. New York, Harper, 1949.

79. STOUFFER, Samuel A. *et al. The American soldier*. 2 vols. Princeton, N.J., Princeton University Press, 1949.

80. SZADZ, Thomas S. *The myth of mental illness*. New York, Harper, 1961.

81. TAUBER, E. S. *and* GREEN, M. R. *Prelogical experience*. New York, Basic Books, 1959.

82. THORPE, W. H. *and* ZANGWILL, O. L. *eds. Current problems in animal behavior*. New York, Cambridge University Press, 1961.

83. WILLIAMS, Norman P. *The ideas of the fall and of original sin*. London, Longmans, Green, 1927.

84. WINNICOTT, D. W. *Collected papers.* New York, Basic Books, 1957.

85. WINNICOTT, D. W. 'Metapsychological and clinical aspects of regression within the psychoanalytical set-up.' In *Collected Papers.* New York, Basic Books, 1957.

86. WINNICOTT, D. W. 'Reparation in respect of mother's organised defence against depression.' In *Collected Papers.* New York, Basic Books, 1957.

87. WYNNE-EDWARDS, V. C. *Animal Dispersion in relation to social behaviour.* New York, Hafner, 1962.

Index

159

Index

Fairbairn, W. R. D., 24, 129, 135

Family, influences of, 142-4

Fantasies, 53, 90, 97, 98, 107, 111, 112, 128, 129, 138; infant, 99, 100; punitive, 99; unconscious, 99-100

Federn, Paul, 141

Forgiveness, 116

Forgotten Language, The, 20

France, psychoanalysis in, 48-9

Free Man's Worship, A, 92

Free will, 16, 132

Freud, Anna, 136

Freud, Sigmund, 9, 14, 20, 23-9, 46, 49, 63, 64, 65, 86, 91, 93, 96, 97, 101-2, 106, 111, 113-14, 116-17, 119-48; agnosticism of, 27; and cosmology, 88-9; and culture, 39-40; and myths, 26-7; and principle of psychic determinism, 12-14; and the problem of meaning, 21; and sexuality, 34; and Words of Power, 33; antagonism to religion, 21-2, 86, 87, 90, 106; neglect of anthropology, 40; on Hebrew/Christian myths, 116; on traumatic neuroses, 16; 'Project' of, 120; pychoanalytic theory of, 31

Freud/Jung debate 111-15

Fromm, Erich, 20, 28

Galileo, 86, 87, 89

Genital character, 34, 38

Genitality, full, 65-6

Gestures, 18, 19, 20

Gilmour, John, 92

Gorer, Geoffrey, 8, 23-50

Great Opportunity, 94

Great System of the World, 89, 92, 94, 105

Greed, 140

Green, M. R., 20

Groddeck, Georg, 22

Growth, human, 135

Guilt, 86, 148; sense of, 17

Guntrip, Harry, 22

Habit training, 44n.

Hartmann, Heinz, 122

Health, concepts of psychological, 65-7

Hegelianism, 49

Heidegger, 122

Heider, 146-7

Heredity, 44

Heterosexuality, 34-5

Hitler, Adolf, 42, 46

Home, H. J., 120-1

Homosexuality, 60, 71

Horney, Karen, 43

House of Elrig, The, 125-7

Humanism, 93-4

Humanities, the, 22

Hysteria, 60, 73, 137-9

Id, 20, 22, 119, 122, 135, 140-1

Identification, 129-30; projective and introjective, 128

Identity, 122; search for, 67

Immaturity, 35

Impatience, 140

Impotence, 53-4

Independence, false, 130; real, 130

Infantile memory, 130-1; nature, 30, 42-3

Infants, 44-6; care of, 44-5

Index

Psychology, person perception, 146-7; scientific, 12-13
Psychotherapy, 119
Punishment, 99-101
Pursuit of Happiness, 34-5, 36

Racism, 41n.
Rapport, 18-19
Rationality, analytical, 145
Reality, human, 145
Reality principle, 135
Religion, 8, 21-2, 27-8, 40, 74, 86-91, 94-8, 102-18; as a neurosis, 91
Replacement, 78; therapy, 18
Repressed drive, 144
Repression, 131, 134, 140
Reproduction, 70
Resistance, 132
Revenge, 99, 100
Rickman, John, 20
Rigidity, 140
Róheim, Géza, 40n.
Russell, Bertrand, 92-3
Rycroft, Charles, 7-22, 62, 68-9, 141

Sadism, 86; moral, 98-102
Sadistic, 30
Sanity, Madness and the Family, 142-3
Sartre, J.-P., 49, 132, 145
Satan, 110, 118
Schachtel, Ernest G., 141
Schizord position, 45
Schizophrenia, 60, 71, 73-4, 76, 125, 128, 129, 130-1, 137, 147; and the family, 142-4
Science, 8, 22, 92-5
Scientific revolution, 105

Secondary gain of illness, 136-7
Secondary process, 147-8
Self, 122, 123-7; embodied, 124-5; false, 16, 67, 124, 130, 133-7, 138; inner, 124, 131; true, 16, 130-1, 133-7
Self and Others, The, 146-7
Self-actualization, 67
Self-knowledge, 64
Self-realization, 67
Semantics, 14-15, 68
Sex, 8
Sex-urges, 100
Sexual organism, female, 36-8
Sexuality, 33-8, 72, 138-9; infantile, 65
Shakespeare, 29n.
Sharpe, Ella F., 29n.
Sheldon, Dr William H., 30
Sleep, 71
Socrates, 64
Social differences, 44
Social relations, 71
Spiritualism, 73
Spock, Dr, 117
Storr, Dr Anthony, 8, 51-84
Stouffer, Dr S. A., 32 n., 154
Super-ego, 101, 119, 122
Symbolic life, 112-13
Symbolism, 20
Symbols, 50
Symptoms, 10-14, 18, 52-84, 141-2; patient and, 10-12; relief of, 59-63
Szasz, Thomas S., 14, 142

Talking cure, 63
Tauber, E. S., 20
Technology, 93-5

Index